GW01071785

How L___
the Mountains ....

A Journey of the Christian Faith
across the UK

Published by JC Ministries

www.jcministries.org.uk

020 8744 5005

AuthorHouse™ UK Ltd.
500 Avebury Boulevard
Central Milton Keynes, MK9 2BE
www.authorhouse.co.uk
Phone: 08001974150

First published by AuthorHouse 9/30/2009

ISBN: 978-1-4490-2967-8 (sc)

This book is printed on acid-free paper.

authorHOUSE®

Contents

Foreword

For the beginning of this Book this scripture comes to mind, 'How beautiful upon the mountains are the feet of those who bring good news'. Isaiah 52. We have steadily done forty days of travelling taking the Good News of Jesus Christ across the Nation from Stornoway to Penzance and then into London. It has been a privilege to do this and to meet so many people, Christians and non Christians alike.

The wonderful work that is being done by Christians, rooted within their localities, in bringing the Good News to the people is commendable. Gill and Stuart Briscoe are a couple who have taken their Gospel feet all over the world, like many others who are giving up their comfort zones to proclaim the Word. Once Jesus asked His disciples, "Will you leave me". "Where would we go", they answered. They had given up so much to follow Jesus; when He died and rose again they hot footed round their country and the World with their Good News. Isaiah describes Jesus and His death on the Cross, a Man of Sorrows. How like sheep we have gone astray and turned away. That He bore the sin of us all. All written before Jesus was even born. The disciples saw Jesus risen and wrote down what they saw in the Gospels. We have the gift of Jesus either to accept or reject Him. We must take the Gospel out just as those early Christians did to a World that is groaning for the Love of Christ. Jesus went out to the lepers, prostitutes, taxmen, families, in fact anyone who wanted to hear. People came for miles to hear the Good News, it gave them hope in a World that was oppressed by the Romans and full of disease and poverty.

Jesus came out of the synagogue and went among His people to tell them of His Fathers Love for them. It was not easy, for so many like their own way of life of sin. Some of the Pharisees and Sadducees disliked Jesus and the very people He mixed with. In Luke 24 Jesus explains to His disciples about His suffering, raising from the dead and repentance and forgiveness of sins would be preached in His name beginning at Jerusalem. They are His witnesses. When we go to Acts 2 Jesus has died on the Cross and ascended back to Heaven. The Holy Spirit comes down upon the apostles like tongues of fire in Jerusalem, Peter and the others speak in everyone's tongues around them.

Today, just as then, we are asked to give the Good News of Jesus Christ. We have the Word, the Holy Bible and the witnesses who saw Jesus rise from the dead. Our World is a hungry World, looking for answers. When God asks, "Whom shall I send," will we answer, "Lord send me," to go among the homeless, the people who are sick, the drunk, the drug addict, the hurting offspring people of all ages who have been dumped by parents.

When the government and people ask, "What shall we do", are we brave enough to say, "follow Jesus, let me tell Him of His love for you", or do we stay silent as the lost drown in their sins and the World grows worse. Jesus, whatever circumstance He was in, gave the Good News of His Father. Is it not worth to be unpopular to save someone's soul and make this a better country. Jesus' promises to be with us. We can tell our neighbour, family and friends about Jesus and His love for us. What a wonderful gift to receive, the gift of Jesus.

'For God so Loved the World that He gave His One and only Son that whoever believes in Him shall not perish but have eternal life.' John's Gospel 3:16.

Heading to Scotland from London

Wednesday 21 May

Psalm 1

Blessed is the man
who does not walk in the counsel of the wicked
or stand in the way of sinners
or sit in the seat of mockers.

But his delight is in the law of the LORD,
and on His law he meditates day and night.

He is like a tree planted by streams of water,
which yields its fruit in season
and whose leaf does not wither.
Whatever he does prospers.

Not so the wicked!
They are like chaff
that the wind blows away.

Therefore the wicked will not stand in the judgement,
nor sinners in the assembly of the righteous.

For the LORD watches over the way of the righteous,
but the way of the wicked will perish.

New International Version

Today is the day for the beginning of the travel of the 'Journey of the Christian Faith.' We awake early and leave home at 2 o'clock in the morning from London. We seat ourselves into the car and drive off. As we come out of the drive we see two foxes going about their business. The early morning is quiet. The street lights shine out their brightness in the morning's dusk. We pass through the streets as early morning workers slowly walk along the pavements. Gradually as we drive on the traffic builds slowly up with drivers going to work. We see the sun rise, the dawn comes bringing the day into glorious colour, as the moon ebbs away and the sun is in the sky, it's golden haze taking over the moonlit sky. It reminds us of Jesus who came into a World dark with sin, He shone brightly to show us a way out of the darkness into the light and He still does as John so beautifully writes in his Gospel. 'In Him was life, and that life was the light of men. The light shines in the darkness, but the darkness has not understood it.' We enter the World into sin's darkness but by trusting in the Son the darkness of sin ebbs away leaving the darkness of night into the daylight.

We stop for breaks, the roadside cafes are closed as it is still very early. We see people cleaning and preparing for a new day, gradually they open so that we can enter in. Is it not wonderful that we can be forgiven by Jesus if we can clean up our lives and ask Jesus into our lives and prepare each day with Him in prayer, worship, bible study. The day progresses, we see many baby lambs, calves, foals. New Life. We too, can have new life, A new start in Jesus if we ask Him into our lives and start again. The countryside was awash in colours of yellows, greens and reds, what a creator we have in the beautiful flowers, in the green grass adorning the road side. Sadly too, animals die on the roadside as so many try to cross the roads. Birds fly too low, other animals stray or decide that the grass is greener on the other side and die in the process. This reminds us of the Prodigal Son who decides to go his own way and crosses that road because he thinks life is better on the other side but he finds that it is not as he is steeped in sin and almost spiritual death. He re-crosses the road where he is forgiven by God his Father and his life is changed.

We continue our journey and soon we arrived in Scotland after passing through Kendal, the mountain tops high, covered by low clouds hugging them. You can imagine Moses chatting to God on the mountain top and writing down the Commandments as God spoke as if they are in a sitting room with cups of tea, Moses busy scribbling down on the paper with a pen all that God was telling him to give to His people. We now see a sign with the name of William Smith the founder of the Boys Brigade.

We arrive at a place called Green Acres just north of Glasgow, after getting slightly lost, we end up in a paddock. We have a group of bemused stable hands wondering what we were doing there. A lady comes to help, we ring the Bed and Breakfast who between them guide us to the correct destination. We are welcomed by a cat called Beauty who looks like her name.

We settle in and go for a walk and find to our surprise and delight a park full of rare breeds of ducks, geese, rams, donkeys etc. We saw many babies snuggling up to their parents, although sometimes these babies are rejected by their parents and are dependent on human love to to help them through. Sometimes, we too are rejected by our human parents but the promise of Jesus is that He will never leave you or forsake you, Jesus is always there. Our Heavenly Father loves and cares for us even when no-one else will fill the emptiness inside and giving us the strength to carry on with the help of His comforter the Holy Spirit.

Green Acres Bed & Breakfast in Cumbernaud Scotland

We returned to Green Acres and Jesus again showed us encouragement. As we came upstairs to our room, there are a group of men sitting playing musical instruments in the upstairs lounge next door to our bedroom. We ask what they are playing. They are coy, not saying too much. As we go into our room they play Christian songs. Hector Cormack, radio presenter from Cullin FM based in the Isle of Skye, rang to speak to us as they were playing and said that the music was no doubt God's commissioning; this is encouraging.

We speak to another presenter of Isles FM Radio based in Stornoway, Isle of Lewis who was setting up an interview with us on the 1 June. He asked for our choice of song for the proposed programme and we suggested the 'Millennium Prayer' of which we have a copy by Cliff Richard. We have danced to this with our friend Ann. This song is from a show called 'Hopes and Dreams' which was chosen by the late Rev Rob Frost, a Methodist minister who did a ministry called 'Easter People' that encouraged Christians to go out and evangelise to others about Jesus. We were privileged to do this dance for the first time at a local church where Rob came along as the guest speaker, he enjoyed the dance. The 'Millennium Prayer sang by Cliff Richard is ideal for the prayer dance. The 'Millennium Prayer' is the Lord's Prayer in dance, it is another way of the Lord's Prayer being told, this is the prayer Jesus gave when His disciples asked Him to teach them to pray. 'Our Father who is in Heaven, Hallowed be Thy name, Thy will be done, Thy Kingdom come here on earth as it is in Heaven. Give us today our daily bread and forgive us our trespasses. Lead us not into temptation but deliver us from evil ' This is from Luke's Gospel 11:1. Two weeks ago we were invited to dance at the Pentecost Festival at Westminster Central Hall, London. It went down well and a little two year old girl loved it, she danced and then tried to dance with flags twice her size. Jesus touched this little one and others through this prayer dance. There was a passion play set to music which had Christians America with our dance taking place at each end of the play, the play was so effective that people gave their lives to the Lord.

We settle in our room, we see the creation of God through the window in all its splendour, the sheep are baaing, a goat tries to butt an archery board twice which was interesting. Sometimes we too can get angry, frustrated and have nowhere to turn. David when chased by King Saul was alone and had no-one to turn to but God. He trusted God, God loved him, the psalms of David cry out to God. "Where can I go? You are in the depths, the heights." He hid in a cave until God gave him the throne and David's descendants would bear the anointed one, the Messiah Jesus Christ, who will reign on His Throne forever.

As we look out of the window we are reminded of Genesis, 'God saw all that He had made and it was very, very good, and there was evening and there was morning the sixth day.' Genesis 1:31.

Today we have travelled 416 miles

Thursday 22 May

Today we ask Sandra, our hostess, about the group of Christians who are also here in the Bed and Breakfast, it turns out that they are Baptists from Maryland, America helping to repair a local church. We meet Cora an Alsatian and Georgia a Spaniel. We are preparing for an interview at Revival FM Radio with Bill Anderson. Sandra very kindly rang them to make sure that we know where we are going. We arrive at Revival FM Radio fairly early.

Bill introduces us to Bill with the same surname who is also a presenter and he very kindly took us round the studio. It has been beautifully decorated and done by Bill and others into a radio station. It is amazing what Christians do by Faith to bring the Gospel to the local community, it is faith, hard work and praying that God will provide the money. Volunteers play such a vital part in helping the studio so that the station's money is spent where it is needed, reaching their community and perhaps a wider audience. As Bill prepares for his show we meet David from Rob Parson's organisation 'Care For The Family', we chat about families and bereavement, we realise even from our own work, how important a family is. So many families are broken and this can affect the child well into adulthood. For parents losing a child is devastating and they need somewhere to turn, David and others are helping where they can. Rob Parsons speaks of the Prodigals, the young people who leave home, leaving behind bewildered parents who do not understand what has happened to their child. The Christian parent has the gift of prayer and God our Father listens. Just as He waits for His children to return to Him, He will listen to our pain and anguish of our lost one. He knows where that child is and their heart. He has been there, when Adam and Eve turned away from Him and went their own way in the garden of Eden. He watched His Son die in agony as He died on the Cross to redeem that what is lost. He knows the joy of a parent when their child returns after a time of suffering. He suffered and suffers as as the parents do. His heart is broken when His children turn away from Him. When a prodigal returns there is a celebration in Heaven with the angels dancing and so it is for our children who have been lost and found welcomed back into the fold.

Colin & Madeleine with Revival FM presenter Bill Anderson

We go into our interview, Jesus inspires us. On the radio news earlier we had heard about young people drinking, in our work we have seen peoples' lives destroyed, their marriages broken, made homeless and sometimes dying at a young age. With the Ten Commandments we can help people to know Jesus and realise that there is an answer that will transform their lives if they desire to know Him.

Our interview ends, David goes in for his interview. Revival FM very kindly supplies us with lunch prepared by Marie, while we are eating our lunch we meet Ann who works for UCB and has come in to do some work with Revival FM. We chat to Ann and Marie then Bill enters, the interview with David is over, David says Good-bye and leaves. Bill sits with us and he chats about

9

the history of Christianity in Scotland. We walk through to the station and we have our photos taken with a member of staff. We enjoy our visit to the studio and go to the shopping centre to buy things we need for the journey. We decide to visit the farm again. We walk through the gate along the pathway towards the fields on our left where there is a donkey and Jacob's sheep which are spotted. We have read that these spotted sheep are the descendants of Jacob's original flock. In Genesis we are told that Jacob was told in a dream by Yahweh to breed sheep from his father-in-law Laban's flock with spots, as they would be stronger and to keep these sheep for himself. Laban had tricked Jacob into marrying Leah his daughter instead of his other daughter Rachael whom Jacob loved. Jacob worked for another seven years for Laban to have Rachael as his wife, God knew how crafty Laban was in getting Jacob working for him and not treating Jacob very well. This was why He spoke to Jacob in the dream. Jacob did well producing sheep from Laban's flock and gained his own flock, then God told him to leave Laban's land taking the spotted sheep with Rachael and Leah, his wives and his children. From Jacob we are reminded of Judah, the son of Leah who becomes the ancestor of Jesus the Christ, the Messianic line. Judah whose offspring came from his daughter-in-law Tamar, their son Perez (meaning breaking out) a twin, came the line of Jesse King David.

Palacerigg Country Park in Cumbernaud

Next to the sheep pen was the donkey and as we look at its back we are reminded of the suffering of Christ. On Palm Sunday as the people proclaimed Him as king, throwing palm leaves down, you can imagine the excitement as the people danced, the adults and the children along the dusty road in front of a man riding on a donkey, singing their praises at the tops of their voices. The donkey we were looking at had the pattern of the cross along his back and down his sides. A dark brown cross contrasting vividly with the lighter brown of his coat, it is said that the donkey bore the pattern of the Cross to remind us that Christ rode on a donkey and died for us on a cross. It also reminds us Next to the sheep pen was the donkey and as we look at its back we are reminded of the suffering of Christ. On Palm Sunday as the people proclaimed Him as king, throwing palm leaves down, you can imagine the excitement as the people danced, the adults and the children along the dusty road in front of a man riding on a donkey, singing their praises at the tops of their voices. The donkey we were looking at had the pattern of the cross along his back and down his sides. A dark brown cross contrasting vividly with the lighter brown of his coat, it is said that the donkey bore the pattern of the Cross to remind us that Christ rode on a donkey and died for us on a cross. It also reminds us that Yahweh (God) promised King David that a descendant would always be on the throne and that person was Jesus, Kings of Kings, Lord of Lords.

We go back to Green Acres, we again marvel at the view from our window of the land, the trees, the animals. We saw the ram busily eating and a group of young men with bows and arrows walking with a tutor to practise archery on the archery board. In this scene you can imagine King David and his men fighting with their bows and arrows. A squirrel is in the tree, first at the top, then the squirrel runs down the trunk, watching this you are reminded of God our creator and as it grew dark, how God came down as Jesus and gave us light in the darkness of this world. Our Bright Morning Star.

Friday 23 May

We pack and tidy our things all ready to go, we go down to breakfast and there we meet the party of Americans from Maryland, they are on fire for the Lord, it is wonderful to chat with fellow Christians, one of whom is a pastor. Our Christian friends pray for us, for the Journey, encouraging us. We pray for their work in Scotland. Photographs are taken. We say farewell to our friends and prepare for the next part of the journey.

As we think about our Christian friends, it is wonderful to think that no matter where we are we can meet Christians like ourselves and that we are as one. We can remember Jesus praying for His disciples, "Let them be one Father, just as we are one." The disciples were very different men, Peter a very enthusiastic man jumping in with both feet. Luke a doctor, working things out, a thinking man, John a poetical man who wrote the beautiful Gospel of Jesus being the Light, how this Light shone in a World of hopelessness and

11

despair. A land taken over by Romans who brought their gods and their ways into a country which was waiting for a saviour, a man who was described as ordinary in looks, nothing to commend him. A man of sorrows, Isaiah 53;

Who has believed our message
and to whom has the arm of the LORD been revealed?
He grew up before him like a tender shoot,
and like a root out of dry ground.
He had no beauty or majesty to attract us to him,
nothing in his appearance that we should desire him.
He was despised and rejected by men,
a man of sorrows, and familiar with suffering.
Like one from whom men hide their faces
he was despised, and we esteemed him not.
Surely he took up our infirmities
and carried our sorrows,
yet we considered him stricken by God,
smitten by him, and afflicted.
But he was pierced for our transgressions,
he was crushed for our iniquities;
the punishment that brought us peace was upon him,
and by his wounds we are healed.
We all, like sheep, have gone astray,
each of us has turned to his own way;
and the LORD has laid on him
the iniquity of us all.
He was oppressed and afflicted,
yet he did not open his mouth;
he was led like a lamb to the slaughter,
and as a sheep before her shearers is silent,
so he did not open his mouth.
By oppression and judgement he was taken away.
And who can speak of his descendants?
For he was cut off from the land of the living;
for the transgression of my people He was stricken.
He was assigned a grave with the wicked,
and with the rich in his death,
though he had done no violence,
nor was any deceit in his mouth.
Yet it was the LORD's will to crush him and cause him to suffer,
and though the LORD makes his life a guilt offering,
he will see his offspring and prolong his days,
and the will of the LORD will prosper in his hand.
After the suffering of his soul,
he will see the light of life and be satisfied ;

> by his knowledge my righteous servant will justify many,
>   and he will bear their iniquities.
> Therefore I will give him a portion among the great
>   and He will divide the spoils with the strong,
>   because he poured out his life unto death,
>   and was numbered with the transgressors.
>   For he bore the sin of many,
>   and made intercession for the transgressors.

New International Version

How rich the Bible is, in showing us a King, in Majesty, beautiful beyond measure. Psalm 22 describes Jesus so well on the Cross.

> My God, my God, why have you forsaken me?
>   Why are you so far from saving me,
>   so far from the words of my groaning?
> O my God, I cry out by day, but you do not answer,
>   by night, and am not silent.
> Yet you are enthroned as the Holy One;
>   you are the praise of Israel.
> In You our fathers put their trust;
>   they trusted and you delivered them.
>   They cried to You and were saved;
>   in You they trusted and were not disappointed.
> But I am a worm and not a man,
>   scorned by men and despised by the people.
>   All who see me mock me;
>   they hurl insults, shaking their heads:
> "He trusts in the LORD;
>   let the LORD rescue him.
>   Let Him deliver him,
>   since he delights in Him."
> Yet You brought me out of the womb;
>   you made me trust in You
>   even at my mother's breast.
> From birth I was cast upon You;
>   from my mother's womb You have been my God.
>   Do not be far from me,
>   for trouble is near
>   and there is no one to help.
> Many bulls surround me;
>   strong bulls of Bashan encircle me.
>   Roaring lions tearing their prey
>   open their mouths wide against me.

I am poured out like water,
and all my bones are out of joint.
My heart has turned to wax;
it has melted away within me.
My strength is dried up like a potsherd,
and my tongue sticks to the roof of my mouth;
you lay me in the dust of death.
Dogs have surrounded me;
a band of evil men has encircled me,
they have pierced my hands and my feet.
I can count all my bones;
people stare and gloat over me.
They divide my garments among them
and cast lots for my clothing.
But You, O LORD, be not far off;
O my Strength, come quickly to help me.
Deliver my life from the sword,
my precious life from the power of the dogs.
Rescue me from the mouth of the lions;
save me from the horns of the wild oxen.
I will declare Your name to my brothers;
in the congregation I will praise you.
You who fear the LORD, praise him!
All you descendants of Jacob, honour him!
Revere him, all you descendants of Israel!
For he has not despised or disdained
the suffering of the afflicted one;
he has not hidden his face from him
but has listened to his cry for help.
From You comes the theme of my praise in the great assembly;
before those who fear You will I fulfil my vows.
The poor will eat and be satisfied;
they who seek the LORD will praise him—
may your hearts live forever!
All the ends of the earth
will remember and turn to the LORD,
and all the families of the nations
will bow down before Him,
for dominion belongs to the LORD
and He rules over the nations.
All the rich of the earth will feast and worship;
all who go down to the dust will kneel before him—
those who cannot keep themselves alive.
Posterity will serve Hm;

future generations will be told about the Lord.
They will proclaim his righteousness
to a people yet unborn—
for He has done it.

New International Version

Jesus came and picked His disciples, an unlikely assortment who came together in faith just as we do. When we meet fellow Christians we have a oneness, a faith in Christ. Our friends came from America but we are one in Christ.

We take down our luggage and we say farewell to Sandra, hubby, Beauty, Cora and George. We set off on our journey to Ullapool. The roads are very smooth in Scotland which helps our journey. We had been thinking about scripture, about Moses going up to Mt Sinai the second time. We pass mountains still iced with snow, covered in mist at the top and sheep at the bottom reminding us that Moses had been a shepherd tending his sheep when God called him to be leader. We had looked at scripture noticing a difference between the first and second time that Moses went up the mountain. The first time the Lord spent seven days on the mountain. His glory around the top, the seventh day red flames appeared. The book of Genesis speaks about Yahweh creating the world in six days, on the seventh day He rested. In Exodus 31:17 God speaks to Moses on the mountain of how He created the Heavens and the Earth and on the seventh day He rested, creating the Sabbath. Moses went up the mountain where Yahweh gave him the Ten Commandments on stone, Moses stayed there for forty days and forty nights, he carried the tablets down the mountain. Sadly for Moses the Israelites had decided as Moses was not around that they would worship a golden idol. Encouraged by Moses' brother Aaron, the Israelites had melted down the gold jewellery that the Egyptian women had given to them as gifts when they left Egypt and created the golden idol. When Moses came down the mountain and saw what had happened his temper went, he broke the tablets in anger. He had to go back up the mountain, this time to chisel out the two stone tablets himself, spend another forty days and forty nights up Mt Sinai. It is interesting to note that in the first book of the Bible, Genesis, Adam and Eve rebelled in the garden after God's creation of six days by eating the apple as soon as God told them not to eat the apple of the tree of the knowledge of good and evil in the garden. The Israelites rebelled and worshipped a golden calf when Moses went up on the mountain the first time, the seventh day. At last the Commandments were ready, Moses came back down the mountain. To a more sober people. The mountains look like a giant finger that has been dipped in paint and gone across the mountains with patterns, a wonderful reminder of God and His creativity. The waters gushing over stones running into rivers. We passed a field with sheep, somehow four sheep had managed to go through a hole and standing on a grass verge looking at the hole in the fence unable to get back in. No wonder scriptures say that we are like sheep who have gone astray. Sheep have one sheep in front whom they will follow in a line, they rely on that sheep to lead them. Sometimes that sheep will err, the others continue to follow just as those sheep did ending up where they should not be, waiting for the shepherd to guide them back. Jesus can guide us back onto the right path, we too can err, follow the wrong crowd, getting deeper into sin but He patiently brings us back into the fold where we belong, forgiven, safe, secure.

We arrive in Ullapool and have a break and go to our next bed and breakfast. Our room is on ground level, the view of the sea, mountains, houses is awesome. We then have a walk into town, we find the people friendly, we go back to the bed and breakfast, the view through our window of the sunset is beautiful with the rays of the sun coming through the sky. A perfect end to a perfect day.

We have travelled 214 miles today to Ullapool.

Saturday 24 May

This morning we load our car and saying good-bye to Shirley our hostess, heading off to the ferry to go to Stornoway. Parking our car in a queue going for a walk in the town before returning to the car. There is a small market with four stalls, a man is serving farm produce wearing his kilt. The town is small, with some shops opposite the quay.

Travelling by ferry from Ullapool to Stornoway

16

There is a small teashop and a shop selling Scottish clothes. All too soon it is time to go back to the car. We drive onto the ferry behind a queue of lorries and cars. We leave our car in the hull. The ferry is big, it has four stories with two cafes and a bar on the first and second floors. The lower top is open decked so you can sit looking out to the sea. We find a settee on which to lie or sit depending on how you feel, many people start to recline. There is a mixed bunch of people of all ages. Some are on holiday, some are people visiting their families, others travelling to and fro from Stornoway.

The Captain greets everyone on board explaining about safety procedures and hopes that everyone will enjoy our journey. The ferry moves forward and we are on our way to the Outer Hebrides. Some people have binoculars, others go and have sandwiches, crisps with tea, while children play. There is a dog playing with two little girls on the floor while their mother watches. Passing the islands, many people are hoping to catch sight of dolphins. We chat to a teacher who is a musician and he knows London as he has worked there. The sea passage is 42 nautical miles (48.3 miles) and as we pass the Islands the sea is sometimes rather rough owing to cross winds from the north sea. We go downstairs to the cafe, it feels like rock and roll, we rock and the ship rolls.

We go back upstairs to the top deck for some fresh air and sit down on the chairs. Soon the Island of Lewis is in view. As we look we can relate this trip to Jesus who many times walked beside the sea of Galilee and sailed on the water, the sea of Galilee can look beautiful and then as suddenly have bad storms. Is not life like this sometimes calm, peaceful then suddenly something happens and our lives are changed. We can feel isolated, scared, alone. We can pray and Jesus will bring us through these times of trial making us stronger in the end. One day Jesus and His disciples went out in the boat, Jesus had a cushion and fell fast asleep in the boat with His head on the cushion. A mighty storm suddenly came up and the disciples felt afraid. The winds and waves went over the boat. Jesus was fast asleep seemingly unaware of the storm. The disciples panicking woke Him up. Jesus stood up and commanded the winds and waves to stop, the weather changed and became calm. The disciples were amazed. "who is this man?" They asked "Even the winds and the waves obey him." They realised then that Jesus was more than a man, that He was God.

When we are feeling alone, afraid, Jesus is there. He comes with us through the still waters of life, through the choppy waters of life back to the calm. With our feet firmly back on the ground, strengthened, refreshed ready to face life again. We go downstairs, and say good-bye to our friend and we set off for our car. We drive out of the ferry into Stornoway, the principal town of Lewis, the next stage of our journey. We go to the next bed and breakfast, we get lost and a lady very kindly gives us directions as the bed and breakfast is about five miles further up the road. We arrive at the bed and breakfast where we meet Donna with her husband Jeffrey. Donna shows us to our room. We tidy up and then drive down the windy road to the town of Stornoway which is to be our contact base for the next few days. We have a look round the town and look for the Church which meets in the Town Hall. We shop in the local Co-Op and have refreshments in the local Arts Cafe. We return to the bed and breakfast. We look at the computer, Sarah has contacted us from the New Wine Church and they have invited us to dinner tomorrow, we are hoping to go to Sarah's Church tomorrow. There is a lovely view of trees and sheep in the fields so near that you feel you could reach out and touch them. We are again reminded of Jesus being the shepherd. In Israel the sheep have names and they follow their shepherd as they know their names, the shepherd has a staff and with the rounded end of the staff gently pulls them back into the fold. We have a Shepherd who cares for His sheep, He knows our names, when we go wrong, He gently brings us back and forgives us when we are sorry for what we have done. He is a forgiving God who loves us if we will confess our sins and turn to Him.

We retire to bed with this thought in mind. We are looking forward to meeting Sarah, her parents Donnie, Catriona and the New Wine Church tomorrow.

We have travelled 52 miles by ferry from Ullapool to Stornoway.

Sunday 25 May

We have a good night, and are moving to another bed and breakfast for one night and we are hoping to meet Neil for a key as we are unable to stay Sunday night in Donna's and Jeff's bed and breakfast. The car is loaded, Donna has very kindly allowed us to leave our large luggage downstairs in the lounge while we go to church and come back to collect it for the other bed and breakfast. We meet a family at breakfast, mum, dad and teenage daughter who have brought their bikes with their car, they have come with friends who are at another bed and breakfast they are hoping to do some cycling while they are here. The roads are smooth and well looked after. Colin set forth on breakfast with corn flakes but suddenly realising that he had ordered porridge, so he eats both. We chat with the family of three.

We leave the bed and breakfast and travel to the New Wine Church in Stornoway. We park and find the Church easily. We walked pass one shop which sells Harris Tweed. The Council is doing the pavement outside the Town Hall, it is fenced in as the work has not yet completed. We walk into the Town Hall and receive a warm welcome, the Church is filled with lively people. The hall is long and there is a balcony behind us and a stage as we look to the front, there were various shields around the hall, what is very interesting is that the shield above the stage has three fishes, a boat and a castle.

The three fishes reminded us of the story of the two fishes and five loaves the feeding of the five thousand. One day Jesus had gone to the hills, the people had travelled far and wide to hear His stories. The day was hot and dusty. They sat, listened for a long time to Jesus and then realised that they were hungry. He put them into groups of hundred and fifties, He asked if anyone had food (the disciples suggest that the people go and buy their own food). A young lad came with two fishes and five loaves. The disciples felt that they would never be able to feed everyone on that amount. Jesus prayed and blessed the bread and it was multiplied. The hungry people were fed that day, Jesus has a lesson here, if we have faith as a mustard seed it will multiply. If we can tell people about Jesus, they come to know Him and they tell others, then many will come into His Kingdom. The mustard seed is a tiny seed which grows into a big tree.

We are greeted by Sarah of the New Wine Church and then sit down. The Service is filled with the Glory of the Lord. The songs spoke of the love of Jesus. Colin speaks to the Church about the Journey of the Christian Faith, Jesus was touching us in a mighty way. Donnie the pastor has been given a gift of teaching and preaching, he is being greatly used by God. People go forward to the front where they are slain in the Spirit, they fall to the floor. God ministered to them in His own way. It was a wonderful Service and afterwards we chatter to people. We arrange to meet Donnie and Catriona when we move our things to the other bed and breakfast.

We head back to Donna and Jeffrey to pick up our things. The weather here has been very warm. We pass beautiful hedges of yellow flowers shining brightly. There are many lambs with their mums in the fields. The Lochs are so blue, they are crystal clear. The mountains are high and when the mist comes down it is like fine linen that has been dropped around their tops and floating slowly down like a long garment.

We find the area for the bed and breakfast, ending up at a block of council flats, we then realise that the bed and breakfast is opposite. We find out afterwards from Donnie that these flats were once lived in by lighthouse keepers who used to man the lighthouse until it became automated, now they are Council property for tenants. We find the bed and breakfast opposite. Neil is waiting for us and gives us a key. We unload our things, tidy up and sallied forth to Donnie and Catriona's home. We come to their road and find a house named 'Shalom' and knock, then we realise that it is not Donnie's and Catriona's home. We see another house in the distance with coaches outside, we drive down and see people come out. We have found the right place and are given a warm welcome. We find that the other house we went to belonged to Catriona's mother. Donnie drives the coaches on school runs with his mother-in-law round the island.

The dinner is superb. It was cooked by Catriona, her daughters and others, the meal is enjoyable and we feel part of the Church family. We go into another room and chat, all too soon it was time to go to the evening Service at Barvas on the the west Side of the Isle of Lewis. This was to us an exciting prospect at Barvas because this was the area of the 1949 revival led by Duncan Campbell where people fell down in the fields while many others rushed into his Church which is in the area. We have two passengers to show us the way to Barvas. One is a young lady from America who found the Lord assisted by a Christian youth worker, who as her neighbour lived two doors away from her home. We pass many sheep. Two have strayed into the road and hastily move when they see us. We have a few problems with cattle grids, being townies we are not used to them so there are a few bumps. We notice that there are lots of stone houses being left to crumble rather than being maintained or being rebuilt. There are now many new houses. Donna told us she had grown up in the stone house next door to their bed and breakfast. Donna and Jeffrey had the bed and breakfast house built next door and did the decorating themselves They have now bought another piece of land next door with the view of building another house for when they retire. Jeffrey grew up in Hounslow, west London, his father a Scotsman came to Hounslow as a soldier and met his English mother. Donna knows Hounslow very well and all the changes: it is indeed a small world considering this is our home town!

We arrive at the Community Hall, pastor Donnie greets us, he points yonder to the Church where the Scottish Revival happened in 1949. As we go through the entrance, we turn left ad sit down, there are windows looking out to the fields. As we look, we imagine the people falling in the fields in the Revival. The Service started and pastor Donnie's gift of teaching comes forth and the Lord sets it alight with the fire of the Holy Spirit, the worship flows and we are touched. Two of our favourite songs " We Walk By Faith," You Set My Feet Dancing" come forth and a lady does a beautiful dance to the music. The service ends all too soon and it is time to leave. We leave the Church and go to look at the Church where the revival happened, we imagine that we are in those days hearing the preaching and the people falling down just as they did this morning in Stornoway. We drive back to our bed and breakfast go into our room, we have a beautiful view of the Loch, we are feeling tired but happy.

Monday 26 May

Today we vacate the bed and breakfast, we have had a good nights sleep, we could see the loch from our window. The daylight hours are long here, it seems strange sleeping and waking up in the night to semi darkness as you do not need to use the lights much. In London it is dark by about 10.30pm at this time of year. We go down to breakfast, we are served by a student who is studying here, there too is a young chef. Colin again forgot he had ordered

20

porridge, he is eating cereals when the porridge is served. We chat to a couple from Bristol who are exploring around these areas and are enjoying their stay. After breakfast, we pay the proprietors as we prepare to leave our room, a knock comes on the door, we have to do another cheque as the amount is not quite right on the first one.

We set back to the other bed and breakfast, we are lost, eventually we knock on a door of a house, the man who is looking after the house for his son gives us directions as best as he can. We find the bed and breakfast placing our things back into the bedroom. We set forth to Stornoway town with our banner. The day is windy, we park near a Co-op and asked if we could display the banner outside the shop but it is not considered ideal. We decide to stand on the grass verge near the kerb. The banner goes up for all to see on a street corner as the cars go past. A man comes along and he starts to chat looking at the 'Ten Commandments' . He worries about us as we hold the banner but we reassure him that we are all right and that the wind is not too strong. Esther from the New Wine Church comes along, we chat then Esther heads off. We stay for about an hour outside the Co-op then folding up our banner we walk to Stornoway Town putting our banner up in a road called Cromwell Street, the leaflets are put on a stand. We are introduced to Esther's husband. People stand and look at the banner. Christians come along, they introduce themselves to us, they pray for the Journey, We meet Esther again. At round 1pm we go the Father's House. Esther and her mum show us where the Father's House is. We go to McKinnons the bakers next door and then to the Father's House.

The Father's House is a meeting house in a building where Christians have fellowship together chatting, eating, etc. There are volunteers who do a rota each day to do the cleaning, tidying up, welcoming visitors. People come in from other denominations which is good for unity. We meet Sarah, and chat with Esther's mum Anne who has been a Salvationist (Salvation Army) all her life, she plays the piano. Esther's daughter Elizabeth or Lizzy as she likes to be known is hoping to join the navy as she loves the sea. After a nice time at the Father's House we set off to find a cafeteria for a dinner of jacket potatoes, while we are searching we see two Christian bookshops which we keep in mind. The first cafe is closed, we see a newspaper office and decide go in. We meet a reporter called Iain, his dad is a Christian and a musician. We realise that we had seen Iain looking at the banner outside when we were on the streets. Iain may be covering for his newspaper relating to local churches outreach taking place on Saturday. We say farewell to Iain and continue our search for a cafe and find one, the lunch is nice. We then go to the two Christian bookshops. The first one we enter has been open for many years. We introduce ourselves to the lady who is serving, and offer her a leaflet about the Christian Journey, which she takes, then we say good-bye. The second Christian bookshop was Blythswood, we enter the shop, we chat to another Iain, we hand Iain a leaflet about the Journey. We see a bookmark with the Ten Commandments which we buy, we say good-bye to Iain and walk to our car, we go to the bed and breakfast then we return to Stornoway town to meet Sarah and the youth group at the Father's House to discuss the outreach on Saturday which will be in the town centre. The evening goes well. Donnie and Catriona arrive, we have wonderful time of worship to the Lord. All too soon we say our good-byes to everyone, we drive back to the bed and breakfast.

We look back over the day, it was successful. When we think of the Father's House we think of Jesus who went out to the people to chat and mingle with them. He ate, feasted, chatted, taught amongst them, just as He does today. His promise is that he will never leave us nor forsake us and we can carry that message today to the streets to the lonely, forsaken, despairing people who have no hope but we can give them the message of the Gospel with the joy and love of forgiveness that only Jesus can give.

Tuesday 27 May

After speaking to the family of three over breakfast we set forth with our banner. We go back to the grass verge near the Co-op. Esther comes to see us, we have a good blether as the Scottish say. Esther was waiting for her husband Bill to go shopping, as she was staying with her mum in the town. Bill's bus has broken down, so Esther is staying with us until he arrives. Bill duly arrives, they set off shopping. After a while we walk to Stornoway, the weather is hot. We have been very fortunate so far as the past few weeks in Scotland have been like this. In the South East we have not had the weather that Scotland has, usually it is the other way round. The wind has not been so blowy today. We set our banner in Cromwell Street which is quite interesting as when one thinks of Oliver Cromwell who was zealous to purify the church, to the point of vandalising the churches. He destroyed organs, carpentry, windows etc. in the churches where men had used their skills, which seems ironic when you think of Jesus being a carpenter. Oliver Cromwell as part of the Puritan movement managed to take out the joy of Christianity, it became a very severe type of religion. We remember men and woman being covered in black. Men with hats and woman with bonnets and aprons over their black dresses. Dancing was forbidden. Life in general was bleak. Christmas day people were not allowed to celebrate Christmas in church and were fined if they did. We are so fortunate to go to Church on Christmas day if we so wish. Today we can go to the church of our choice and worship in the way we are happy with.

Jesus never wanted Christianity to be joyless, He was born a Jew and lived as one of the people, He danced, He learnt, He had brothers and sisters. His mother taught Him about His Father God (Yahweh) His earthly father Joseph taught Him to be a carpenter so that He could make a living. He went to the synagogue, He worshipped there. He then began His ministry at the age of thirty. He saw the way the Pharisees and Sadducees, the religious people were behaving. They were Zealous Jews who had become so religious that that they had lost their love and compassion for the people that they were supposed to help and teach about God. If anyone touched them, they were tainted by that person, they would immediately wash their clothes, they were so fastidious, they were always washing their hands up to their elbows. They would walk through the street carefully avoiding the 'riff raff', making rules so rigid for people that they could not keep them.

John the Baptist who was baptising in the River Jordan for the baptism of repentance had stern words for them, he pointed at the Sadducees and Pharisees by the River Jordan calling them a brood of vipers. He was telling them that they were doing religion but on the inside like the rest of us that they were sinners. Jesus spoke too, that out of our hearts can come evil thoughts through our words and actions, like envy, murder, greed, it is not what we look like on the outside it is what we are on the inside. God can see inwardly. Man cannot do this. Jesus also said that by their fruit you shall know them. You will know a Christian who follows Jesus rather than a person who does what man tells him. "Be ye transformed by the renewing of your mind," Paul says in Romans 12:12, this is true for you can go to church for years, you may have not faith, you can become a Pharisee with little love in your heart for those round you who have fallen, inside the church, and for those who are outside it.

Chatting to passers by on the streets of Stornoway

We wait with our banner, some people look but not coming too near. Two Christians come up and speak to us because Jesus had told them to, they come form local churches, they pray for us. One lady comes up, she gives us

23

chocolate which she has bought in Woolworths, we thank her. We meet another lady from the New Wine Church who has a gifting in fostering children who have been emotionally disturbed, she has done a great job with them. Christians from the New wine Church say "Hello" as they pass. While we are here a lady is playing the bagpipes, she is very good. She has finished college and is going round different countries busking until she is ready to settle. She has just come back from New Zealand, she earns enough money to pay her way, she comes from a musical family.

At 1 o'clock we rolled up the banner, we go to the Fathers House. We have a warm welcome, we settle in and chat. We play with a little boy called Gavin, he is about eighteen months old, he is very bright and good at football. We speak to Anne and Esther, they are off to Esther's house to stay. We leave the Fathers House and go to do some shopping, we return to the bed and breakfast.

In the evening there is a massive fire which spreads across the hills, it comes up in thick blankets of smoke, fire engines come to the road, the fireman get out and look. As the evening grows into dusk you can see the glow of the fires, cars, the hills. The weather has been very hot here, it has dried the grass on the hillsides making them like a tinderbox ready to be set alight at any time.

The fires remind us of Pentecost when the Holy Spirit came down, there were tongues of fire settling on the people, small fires ready to set the World ablaze with the Great fire of the Holy Spirit, the beginning of Christianity.

Wednesday 28 May

The day is blowy and wet, over breakfast we meet two young people, a man from Spain and a lady from Germany. We speak of the housing crises in Spain, the lack of jobs for builders. The Global Crunch is affecting us all. Germany it seems does not have the tourist industry that Spain has. The Rhine is a beautiful river to visit, people can have trips on the River Rhine. We speak of Barcelona. The young man is leaving today, he has travelled quite a few times to Britain, he likes rugby, all too soon breakfast was over, we have enjoyed our conversation. We decide to have a walk along the fields for ten minutes. Colin decided that it would be a good idea to walk into a field of sheep, I am not so sure. There are no pavements here, so we walk along the road, we open the gate and enter the field shutting the gate behind us. The sheep looked at us in astonishment, moving away as fast as they could, there is a river running in the field, a ram pokes his head up from the river bank, we decide to leave and forget our walk.

We drive to Stornoway, it is quite wet today, we go straight to the High Street and set up our banner. People come up chatting to us. Opposite us is a pub where a starling is flying in and out of a hole where it is feeding it's young. While we are standing here two men come along with a ladder, the lady from the pub comes out with a cardboard box from which there is cheeping. The men take the box, one climbs up the ladder, he puts a little starling back into the wall. Colin asked what had happened, it turns out that the little bird had fallen out of its nest and into the pub lady's lounge in her flat above the pub. She rang two friends to put the starling back. The parent bird continues going in and out as though nothing has happened.

Jesus reminds us about the birds when mentioning sparrows. They used to sell five sparrows in the markets for two pennies. Yet God does not forget His sparrows. Jesus speaks to us, saying how precious we are, that we are of more worth than sparrows. He looks after us just as that starling looked after its young. Luke 12:6. He feeds us just as that starling fed its young and made that nest for its young. The baby starling fell out, he was lost. Just as we can go wrong in sin, the Father waits . We turn away but we can say sorry, we are forgiven, we are gently put back into that nest lovingly by Jesus as if we have never been away.

A gentleman comes to speak to us, he was from the Scottish Church, he had been a butcher, we spoke of the revival in 1949 on the Isle of Lewis in the Outer Hebrides led by Duncan Campbell. He prays for us. People come, they look at the Ten Commandments and our leaflets are taken. Another lady from the New Wine Church comes to speak to us with her two sons, she very kindly buys us some tea and sandwiches. She is a wonderful mum with three autistic sons and loves them with a great love, she is arranging a birthday party for one yet she very kindly gave what she could to buy us food and drink.

Again we can relate to Jesus who was in the temple with His disciples, He watched as people put money into the collection box not worrying too much about it, they had plenty, it was money that they would not miss. When a widow lady came along who did not have much money she placed in all she had, she would miss this money. She was prepared to go without for God's Kingdom while the others put in money that they would not miss. Mark 12:40. Sometimes Jesus asks us to go somewhere for Him, to give up time to do something for Him, maybe give up our favourite television programme to pray for someone. Something we enjoy. Is it not better to see our time profitably spent to see someone to come to know the Lord through our time spent in prayer for others and ourselves. This lady from the New Wine Church gave what she had, we are very grateful for her thoughtfulness and kindness.

At 1 o'clock we fold up our banner, we go to the Fathers' House for fellowship, refreshments. Afterwards we go to the smaller Co-op, shopping. We go back to the bed and breakfast. We rest and travel to the Father's House for a Service. We have a great evening, Donnie's preaching is excellent. We feel that God is going to do a mighty work in Stornoway. Jesus

25

wants His people into His Kingdom. He is knocking at the door, He is preparing His people to be fishers of men and women. It feels such a privilege to be part of this, to see the Christians in Stornoway to be part of this great work.

We were given scripture from Luke 5 about casting the net. Jesus asks Simon Peter, the first disciple of Jesus, to cast a net from his boat. Jesus had been preaching from Peter's boat and when He had finished preaching He asked Peter to go further out in the water and put out his net. Peter had a great catch, he caught so much fish that others came into help, Peter told Jesus to go away from him as he was a sinful man. Jesus said to Peter, "Don't be afraid from now on I will make you a fisher of men."

The Lord is working. He is listening. 'If my people will humble themselves, then I will listen and heal the land.'" 2 Chronicles 7:14, God heard the peoples cries in Egypt, He sent Moses to bring them out of their bondage. Jesus too can bring us out of bondage of sin, He has died on the Cross for us, He was separated from his Father while dying on the Cross but He died that we would be set free from the bondage of sin. Just as Moses led the people out of Egypt, Jesus leads us out of sin. It will not be easy, we will err, but Jesus gives us the strength if we believe and trust in Him. Amen.

We return to the bed and breakfast.

Thursday 29 May

We set forth down to Stornoway by car. We take along with us an umbrella in case it rains. We park our car and walk into Stornoway to Cromwell Street. The morning is interesting. The pub opposite has the Celtic Cross reminding us of early Christianity in Scotland. In England early Christianity from Rome with St Augustine coming to our shores, in the far north of Scotland, Christianity was already there when the Church came from Rome. Scotland and England vary in the history of Christianity. In years to come Presbyterianism came into Scotland and Wales and it was to become the main form of Christianity while in England it was more for the Church of England. In 1689 William of Orange allowed the Church of Scotland to have its own autonomy and became the Presbyterian Church whereas the Church of England was not Presbyterian, so they went their own ways as they are today.

It is an interesting morning, we had prayed to the Lord that it would not rain while we were with the banner, He honoured this prayer. A lady came came up, she had been living in Scotland for five years, she asked about Christian Radio as we have been in contact with a few radio stations in Scotland,

Christian and non-Christian. It turns out that she particularly wanted Premier Christian Radio. We were amazed at this as it is our local station in London where we live. We are so blessed that we can tune into Premier whenever we like. The internet has opened up an arena of Christian stations and non Christian stations who do an output of Christian programmes, we have more choice than we ever had to hear the Gospel.

So spread the Good News Jesus said, the radio has done this, spreading the Good News across the world. Through stations like FEBA who have worked in countries in many parts of the world where people who cannot otherwise hear the Good News. It is important for people to support their local Christian radio stations and Christians who are working in the media. Many Christian Stations rely on volunteers and without whose help they could not continue to broadcast. We need to pray for them and all our Christian presenters, pray that many will come to know the Lord.

We are blessed, a lady comes along, she had been a young woman at the time of the revival in 1949, her eyes shine as she remembers people being touched by the Holy Spirit seeing lives changed. She herself has been a Christian for sixty five years, she could recall the time quite clearly, it was a privilege to be able to see what happened through someone who has lived through this time, how wonderfully the Lord works through people who are willing and never give up praying. What an encouragement for many of us to pray for family and friends to be saved. She prayed for us and then went on her way. The Hebrides Revival started through prayer by two sisters called Christine and Peggy who were daughters of the local minister. They prayed solidly for people to know the Lord.

We meet the lady who came on Tuesday with some chocolate. She gives us some sweets, she is an office worker and has looked us up on the internet. She leaves, Colin went to buy some tea. As he goes to the shop they meet up, she very kindly goes and buys us some tea. God is good! It is a great morning. A couple of traffic wardens come by, then two local policeman. At 1 o'clock we fold up our banner, we walk to the bakery for jacket potatoes. We then go to the 'Father's House', as usual we are made very welcome, we have some lovely chats with the people. There is a small bible study group learning at one of the tables. We enjoy ourselves then we leave the 'Father's House' and go to the small Co-op, then back to the Bed and Breakfast.

We have a lovely view here of the Scottish mountains and loch, every morning there are two bunnies playing in the garden. There are feldfare, blackbirds, chaffinches and a cleft dove. The loch never stays the same, it is beautiful ever changing its colours. The mountains change from moss green to light green as the sun streams across them. The skies are assorted blues. The clouds flow gently across the the sky, they seem never ending.

Jesus promises that He will never leave nor forsake us. When David fled from King Saul he was a fugitive, living in caves. Saul did not like David as David had been chosen by God to be the new King as Saul had disobeyed

God. David had written many psalms to express how he felt but he trusted God (Yahweh) to pull him through. He must have felt frustrated at times unable to stay in one place as Saul was at his heels trying to kill him.

David wrote Psalm 139 to say, "whether I am in the heights or depths, you are there, you are with me." The beautiful Psalm 23 talks of God being our shepherd. That thought consoled him. Jesus too, was to experience what David went through. Jesus came from the line of David. Jesus was the one whom was spoken of by King David, a promise of a King who would reign for ever, King of Kings. Lord of Lords, not an earthly throne but a Heavenly one. Jesus, living in Israel, trusting His Father, putting His life in His hands (trusting Him all the way to the Cross where He died). He did not want to die on a Cross any more than we would, He did it because He loves us so much, a never-ending love so vast and so wide. He went through events as David did, David had to live in a cave. Jesus said "The Son of Man has nowhere to put His head." The Pharisees and Sadducees were like King Saul chasing David, where-ever Jesus went they were there waiting to accuse Him, to criticise what He did. They were always at His heels like Saul with David.

Whatever situation we go through, He is with us, whether we are homeless, lonely, no friends or family to help, in sickness, He loves us, He longs to guide us through. He lowered Himself to become a servant when He washed His disciples feet. Jesus said, "I no longer call you servants but friends." In the Book of Genesis God walked in the garden with Adam and Eve, they were friends, then the Devil came into the garden in the form of a serpent, he broke that friendship, sin came in all its ugliness, severing that bond of friendship with God, man and women. Jesus restored that friendship with His people through His disciples. Wen we ask Jesus into our lives, He is our friend forever, His promise is that He will never leave nor forsake us, Turn to Him when you feel forsaken, He will never let you down.

Psalm 123

A song of ascents.

I lift up my eyes to You,
 o you whose throne is in Heaven.
As the eyes of slaves look to the hand of their master,
 as the eyes of a maid look to the hand of her mistress,
 so our eyes look to the LORD our God,
 till he shows us Hs mercy.
Have mercy on us, O LORD, have mercy on us,
 for we have endured much contempt.
We have endured much ridicule from the proud,
 much contempt from the arrogant.

New International Version

Friday 30 May

Having our breakfast and we chat to a visitor who is moving home in Scotland. He has brought his dog. He has served in the Army. He stayed overnight and leaves early next morning. After breakfast we set off for Stornoway, as usual we park our car and pray. We went forward aware that this is our last weekday talking to people in Stornoway before departing for Skye. We went to our usual place opposite the pub in Cromwell Street. Esther and Annie, her mum come by, little Garath chats to us in his tartan kilt. It is the first time we have seen a little boy in a kilt. The weather is good as it usually is, God has been kind to us. Colin wore his sun hat to protect himself from the heat of the sun. A lady called Sally from the New Wine Church comes and chats with us, she is a new Christian, she is delightful to talk to. She stays with me for a while Colin goes to fetch us a cup of tea. Later we pack our banner away. A gentleman talking to his two friends in the pub doorway comes over, he asks for two leaflets. Colin finds them and gives them to him. We go to the Father's House, then have a potato each from 'Mckinnons' next door. Again we have a great time chatting with everyone and a man called Thomas. We then leave, we walk through the town, we meet a man called Ian from a local church, he takes us to meet Thomas who is the Minister of St Martins Church. We go through the Church doorway, turning left we go into a huge room with posters of the Boys Brigade. The Boys' Brigade was started by Sir William A. Smith in 1883 with a company of thirty young men in Glasgow to teach young men about Jesus and to give them a Christian foundation. Its aim is the advancement of Christ's Kingdom among boys and the promotion of Habit, Obedience, Reverence, Discipline, Self Respect and all that tends towards true Christian Manliness. Many Boys' Brigades are in Scotland, as well as England and world-wide, the Queen is the patron of the Boys' Brigade, they are an excellent training ground for musicians as you can be trained to play bagpipes, drums etc. Ian introduces us to Thomas and leaves. We chat and say farewell, we drive back to the bed and breakfast and refresh ourselves before travelling back to Stornoway town to meet Donnie and Catriona who take us to dinner at the Art's Centre. We have a great time of fellowship. After the meal we go to the Father's House for the evening worship. The prayer time is powerful, we pray for people to be saved. After the service we go out into the streets .

Sarah and the other young ladies dance outside the Father's House with the front window open with the music coming through. We recognised the music which was sung by the Christian group 'Mary, Mary'. The dancing is good. Esther joins us, she points out Cheryl who is one of the dancers, Cheryl was brought to Church by Esther, Cheryl found a faith and was baptised with Esther. The dancing is Jesus inspired, it is very effective. Younger and older people watch the dancing. One young man joins in. After the girls finish the dance they go onto the streets to give the Good News of Jesus.

New Wine Church young people dancing outside the 'Father's House'

Music and dancing play a great part in the Bible, Psalm 149 and 150 speak of dancing and music. King David loved dancing, which sadly caused a rift with his wife Mical. One day he danced in the streets. David took off his kingly robes, he dressed as a servant, just as Jesus did when washing the disciples feet, and danced with all his might. Mical looked out of the window, she did not like what she saw. a king dressed like a servant, what would people think, how disgraceful, he was a king not a servant. She could not see David's love for his Father God, David just wanted to please him, he danced for God. Mical did not see it that way she saw only disgrace, humiliation for herself and David, she did not think of what God thought but man. The Bible says that she despised him. When he came to see her after he finished dancing she rebuked him. The Lord closed her womb, she was never able to have children.

This is a lesson to us all, that a person who comes to the Lord and wants to please Him to show that they love Him while another will come, scoffing pulling the person down. As Colin and I reflect on this I am reminded of something that happened when I was doing some flower arranging in church, I was working in the main church area by the altar, I had to pop downstairs to get something. When I came back a disabled lady had taken some twigs from my pile of flowers on the chair, she had put them into a vase which she placed onto the altar, she was so proud of what she had done, they were wonderful. I thanked her for her flower decoration, she was very happy, It was done out of love, I am sure God was smiling as she left her gift on the altar.

Praise is a wonderful gift. Praise uplifts people when they do well and praising our Lord Jesus is so uplifting. Praise Him in the evening, praise Him in the morning, let everything that has breath, Praise the Lord. (Psalm 50). We leave Stornoway and go back to the bed and breakfast.

We go down to breakfast as usual, we travel into Stornoway. Calum rings to tell us we are on Isles FM Revival tomorrow at 1.30 pm. We have asked him to play the 'Millennium Prayer' by Cliff Richard and 'These are the days of Elijah' by Robin Mark. We go to a restaurant that Donna has suggested to order a meal for tomorrow. We walk round the town and then sit in the sun by the town hall, Donnie comes along, he sits and chats with us, he goes to find Catriona, they come back to us, we insist on taking them to dinner this time to say thank you for their wonderful hospitality and for looking after us so well.

Pastor Donnie & Cartiona with Madeleine in Stornoway overlooking Ferry

We finish our meal and we go to the Father's House, we pray for the outreach and set forth. We meet many Christians from St Martin's Church. We put our banner near Woolworths while the others move further forward from Woolworths to dance. A lady comes along with a snake. People admire and stroke the snake. A crowd gathers to watch the dancing by Sarah and the others. The lady with the snake joins the crowd. The dancing is Christ centred, it is beautiful, people are copying the dancing. An assistant comes out of Woolworths, he asks us to move as we are standing in front of a fire exit. We move nearer to the dancing. A guy who is a Christian comes up and speaks to us, he has a tee shirt with a picture of nails on it. Sarah asks him to join in the dance, to be Jesus on the Cross, not realising the picture on his tee shirt. The dance begins, he comes in, he puts out his arms for Sarah to put the nails in, there is a stunned silence from the crowd, as on each arm as he spread his arms out are the words Jesus Christ. Sarah was astonished, the people are affected by what has happened. The leaflets for the Ten Commandments are taken. The man who was Jesus explained that he had just had the tattoos done. The outreach has been a success and we return to the Father's House very happy. We leave the banner there while we go shopping for Monday as we will be leaving Stornoway early morning. After shopping we have an ice cream and sit in the sun. Sarah opens up the Father's House, we collect our things, we are feeling tired. We go back to the bed and breakfast while Sarah goes back to do another outreach in the street.

We are coming up to the single roadway where there is a traffic jam which is unusual for these roads. A car turns and goes another way. We wait, we can see way out in front a lorry lift truck, a man is walking backwards and forwards across the road. There is a car on the verge belonging to one of people working on the accident. A driver gets out to find out what is happening, we ask him what has happened, he tells us that there has been a terrible accident. We wait and watch as two cars are taken away. The two cars are crushed. A worker comes past on our left and looks at us as he passes, he goes to his car. A police car goes past, we start to move, we pass another police car.

We arrive back at the bed and breakfast and we go in, we hear one of the two dogs barking. We are surprised that Donna and Jeffrey are not in. We go upstairs as usual. We notice out of our window that the lawn in the garden has been cut, the bunnies are playing in the garden, over the past few days the two adult bunnies have brought into the garden their two baby offspring. We settled down for the evening when we hear a voice calling up the stairs. The voice sounds like Donna's, we open the door, Colin calls out Donna but it is not Donna, the voice belongs to Donna's sister. Her sister explains to us that Donna and Jeffrey were in the accident we saw. Donna has been badly injured and has been airlifted to a Glasgow hospital. Jeffrey is in the local hospital with minor injuries. One of their dogs had died in the accident. There were guests coming this evening and we are asked to greet them when they come. The guests duly arrive, we greet them and chat. We then go back to our room.

We think with sadness what has happened, it has been a great shock, we realise that at times like this we can pray and allow the Lord to have His way in this. We pray for Donna and Jeffrey.

Psalm 121 comes to mind ....

A song of ascents.

I lift up my eyes to the hills—
where does my help come from?
My help comes from the LORD,

the Maker of Heaven and earth.
He will not let your foot slip—
    He who watches over you will not slumber;
    indeed, He who watches over Israel
    will neither slumber nor sleep.
The LORD watches over you—
    the LORD is your shade at your right hand;
the sun will not harm you by day,
    nor the moon by night.
The LORD will keep you from all harm—
    He will watch over your life;
the LORD will watch over your coming and going
    both now and forevermore.

End of the first phase of the Journey

Forty Day Journey begins ... Sunday 1 June

Stornoway, in the Outer Hebrides Scotland

Today is a new day. The little dog is missing his owners, a car arrives early in the morning to the house. The place is a hive of activity. We come down to breakfast. Donna's sister and niece are helping, there is another surprise, the lady we met in Stornoway who very kindly gave us sweets on the the outreach is there helping. She has heard about the accident and has come to help, she is a friend of the family. Everyone is helping each other, the guests and the helpers, it is a wonderful thing to see. We all ask how Donna is, she is still very ill in hospital in Glasgow but somehow despite all this there is a feeling of hope, that God was saying don't worry, it will be all right. Jeffrey is coming out today, he wants to come home. We are thankful that he is feeling well enough to come out. We chat to an Italian couple, they come from the mountains of Italy, they are visiting Scotland, they are enjoying their visit. The wife has studied English, she speaks English well, she was easy to understand.

We finish breakfast, we set forth to the Town Hall for a Service hosted by the New Wine Church. We have a great worship time. Colin is asked by Donnie to chat to the congregation which he does. The talk goes well, we ask if people have asked Jesus into their lives. We dance to the 'Millennium Prayer Dance' sung by Cliff Richard, it goes down well especially with the flags. We knew how much the Lord wants this Prayer Dance in His Church, it has as far as we know gone to Korea to testify to a family out there about Jesus. We did this prayer dance with our friend Ann at the first Pentecost Festival in London, started by the late Rev. Rob Frost of Easter People, he was a minister of the Raynes Park Methodist Church. It was an amazing day as it was a Saturday and Pentecost. Our friend Ann wrote on our behalf, Jesus provided two slots for us. Unknown to us a two and a half year old girl was affected by what was happening in the front. The dance consists of a formulated dance, freewheeling and flags. This little one started dancing near us, and was away. Between the two dances was a passion musical play, at the end of the play people gave their lives to the Lord. The actors in the play had come from Florida and were exceptional. The flags were put back after the

34

play and while we were waiting this little one tried to dance with each flag. It was a wonderful sight to see, this little child dancing for Jesus.

When we are in London running our drop-in centre we normally, after the dinner, give a message. An amazing thing happened, bearing in mind that some of the people were not Christians. On the last hymn people were singing as though there was a huge choir. Colin played the piano, it sounded as it never sounded before, a man played the harmonica. A lady and myself danced, she sang as she danced and her voice completely changed. A lady sitting in front of us said that we danced exactly the same. This was similar to what had happened in the book of Acts when the Holy Spirit came down in 'tongues of fire' upon the apostles they were truly changed. It was an extraordinary day.

The first Millennium Prayer Dance we did was in front of Rob Frost, he was able to see it and he enjoyed it. Although we did not know Rob that well we had met him at seminars and Premier Christian Radio. What was amazing was his zest for life and his evangelism. He had this song put into a musical called 'Hopes and Dreams', of which he was part where it was danced by a group of dancers called the 'Springs'. We are so pleased that Jesus has allowed us to do this dance, it is a happy memory of such a nice person who was passionate for Christ.

After the dance we have prayers said for us but we have to rush out of the door for the radio interview. Just as we go out a man calls out to us. He has had a vision, he has a picture of the whole country, the Gospel going far and wide. The Gospel spread into a Cross spreading north, south, east, west. We realise that this meant that all the nations would come into contact across the country, including London as there are many people coming to and fro from across the World. We hurry to the studio to Isles FM. Sarah has contacted Calum Campbell to interview us for his programme, 'I am not ashamed', we record two programmes. Calum is a 'born again' Christian, we pray, the Lord blesses us. The two programmes we do go well. We tuck into their biscuits and tea, Calum asks about Donna and Jeffrey as to how they are. We have our photo taken with Calum, we say good-bye and go to dinner. We are due to return to the Town Hall this evening for the Youth Service which is attended by the youngsters of Stornoway's various churches. After an excellent meal we walk back to our car and we meet the Italian couple from the bed and breakfast, after a chat we sit in our car and wait for people to come. As we wait in the car we see a way of church going which has changed little in Stornoway. The women are wearing long skirts, jackets and hats while the men wear hats. In the United Kingdom for many years women could not wear trousers to church and wore hats. Sarah arrives we go to the Town Hall. The hall is packed with young people of all ages, a man called Charlie who is very evangelical asks Colin if we are the speakers, we say no, but it turns out we are. Sarah has put our names forward to be the speakers. After a few songs we go out front, we speak of our work and the Ten Commandments, it is a great evening, Soon we say our good-byes and leave.

We arrive at the bed and breakfast. Donna's sister is there. Great news Jeffrey is here, he wants to see us. We meet his son-in-law Jeff. Jeffrey comes into the lounge and explains how the accident happened, by God's mercy, he, Donna and a nineteen year old driver in the other car were not killed. They had gone out for the afternoon with their two dogs and decided not to use Donna's smaller car and used the bigger one that they own, which saved their lives. Donna has had an operation, she is improving. We pray for Jeffrey, Donna and the family. We are so pleased to tell him about Jesus the healer and how He loves us.

We say good-bye to Jeffrey, tired but happy we go to our room. We read in the Gospels of Jesus the Healer. the Restorer. In Isaiah 61 we read of the Messiah preaching Good News to the poor. Jesus read this out in the synagogue in His home town of Nazareth and said, "Today this scripture has been fulfilled." He was not popular when reading this out, in fact the people tried to throw Him over a cliff. When John the Baptist was in prison he sent his disciples to ask Jesus if He was the Messiah. Jesus responded, the blind see, the lepers walk, then John knew that Jesus was the Messiah because the Messiah would have the signs of healing.

The Pharisees did not like Jesus having dinner with tax collectors and others and they told Him so, Jesus replied, "I have come for the sick," Mark 2 :17, it is the healthy who do not need a doctor. We are in a fallen world soaked in sin of which illness is a part. Jesus came to free us from that sin and to heal us. The words come to mind. Friend are you saved?

We have travelled around 200 miles in the Isle of Lewis.

Monday 2 June

Today is the start of the Forty Days Journey, we get up at 4.00 in the morning. We move about quietly, we hear a cuckoo in the tree. We take our belongings down the stairs, through the door, we get into the car, unfortunately so have the midgets. They are everywhere. As we start the car we open the windows to let them out. Thankfully they go. We set off for the ferry to the Isle of Skye. We say good-bye to Stornoway and the peat which many people are collecting because of the oil crisis, there is miles of it alongside the sheep. Many sheep are walking along the road, adults and baby lambs, so we have to be extra careful. We arrive early for the ferry and wait. The day is already showing signs of being warm as we wait. There is a motorcyclist who is camping, we chat, he is enjoying his journey round the Island. We move the car into the car park to be ready to go onto the ferry, two cyclists, husband and wife, come down the hill, they wait to board the ferry. Most of us seem half asleep. We hand our tickets to an attendant who is going round collecting them. At last the ferry arrives and we drive on board. We park our car in the hull of the ship and go up the stairs. As we walk away from the stairs there is a little sweet shop in front of us with a lounge on our left, you can see the bow. There is another lounge near the cafe. Also on either side of the ship there are seats in rows like being on a plane. On your left side as you go to the cafe people are sitting there, on the right hand side there is the television with the morning's news programmes. The captain's voice comes across the intercom welcoming us aboard, his assistant takes over explaining about safety, then we are off to the Isle of Sky. The journey is smooth, we are enjoying it. We chat to the two cyclists who are cycling around Scotland. We are all looking at the computer which has a map telling us where we are.

Crossing from Uig Isle of Harris to Skye

We see the Isle of Skye coming into view and get ready to disembark. We go down the stairs back into our car and drive into Skye. As we set forth into Skye we see that Skye is very different to Stornoway, both are very beautiful with the lochs. The lochs change colours with the light from a brilliant blue to grey. The houses seem more Swiss and Austrian, many are coated with white like icing on a cake, it is very green. We see two cows on a grass verge, we slow down to look at them, they look at us in a huff, there seem to be more cows here.

We head towards our bed and breakfast that is in the north west of Skye, about 20 miles from Portree the principal Town. We are early, four hours in fact. We find the bed and breakfast, it is situated in a tiny little village with two pubs, hotels, a pottery and a little convenience store from where the view is quite a sight. The day is hot, we spend our time between the pottery and convenience store while we are waiting to enter the bed and breakfast. We buy a newspaper, a drink, we wait. We look at the view of the water below us, the sheep and the fields and cars passing along the road, it is quite busy. We look at the newspaper which is Scottish, we switch on the radio it is in Gaelic Scottish. We manage to get Radio 4. We visit the pottery and have a look round. It is a working pottery where potters make their wares, glaze and paint them. We asked where their materials come from and were told that they came from Devon. They are listening to Radio 2.

There are pots, lampshades, ashtrays of all shapes and sizes, colours. There are clay pots which reminds us of Jesus and of the changing of water into wine in the stone water pots at a wedding (John 2) when the hosts ran out of wine, Jesus saved the day and the hosts from the embarrassment of having no wine. What a miracle. It reminds us of John baptising with water to make people's sins clean, we remember Jesus shedding His blood on the Cross, His side pierced by the Roman soldiers, water poured out of His side, then blood. In the book of Genesis we read that Moses struck the rock and the water gushed out. Living water for the people to drink, just as Jesus is the living water for us today.

Jesus was in the temple before he died on the Cross. The priest had gone down with the people with a phial to the pool of Siloam. The procession of people would go down to this pool, the priest would fill the phial with water from the pool of Siloam. He would head the procession back to the synagogue, there a lamb was sacrificed, the blood was poured over the altar and the water was mixed. It is believed that around this time Jesus cried out in anguish in the Temple Courts while teaching the people to believe in HIm. John 7 verse 28. The world passes by and does not want the Fountain of Life.

Outside B&B in Skye with proprietor Sandra , member of Skye Bible College

We sit outside the pottery, we go back to the shop, then to the bed and breakfast where we are welcomed by Sandra. We put our things into our bedroom, we change to go to Portree. We drive down the road with the views of the loch. We park in a car park which is in a square, there is a police station with a memorial to World War Two. We take our banner and leaflets out of the car. We walk and pray for a spot to put up the banner. We go into a cafe and have a meal, a man at another table says "hello" to us, after the meal we set off to our spot. We put up our banner outside an empty shop opposite Safeways. We pray for Christians to come and speak to us. Our prayers are answered, we met Tesh the man we had said "hello" to in the cafe. He is from Zimbabwe, he is a chef and a 'born again' believer. He has lived in Romford, London and went to a Pentecostal Church in London. He is now working in Portree High Street where he is doing Christian work with young people. He is hoping to preach in the Church of Scotland after having a chat with the minister.

People come out of Safeways across the road. But they do not come over. We folded up our banner, two children come over to look in the shop window where we are, they say "hello" and go. We go back to the bed and breakfast, we are pleased and surprised to find in the drawer a UCB's 'Word for Today' as many bed and breakfasts do not have a Bible these days. So we feel at home. We have a view of the garden and the loch. We have a read of the People's Friend, We have always loved 'Views from the Manse' which is a Christian feature, seeing the beautiful pictures of Scotland and its Scottish history amongst other things within this excellent paper, to see these views come to life before your eyes is exciting.

We have had a long day, we are asleep as soon as our heads hit the pillows.

We have travelled 35 miles from Stornoway to Uig Ferry, Isle of Harris
We travelled 27 miles from on the Ferry across to Skye
We travelled 16 miles from Skye Ferry at Uig to Portree

Tuesday 3 June

What a surprise, Sandra and Peter her husband are Christians. They have moved from the Midlands to Portree because the Lord had called them, they belong to a Pentecostal Fellowship who have starting the Skye Bible College. They know Donnie and Catriona and Sarah. The youth are going to 'Frenzy', an event for the young in Edinburgh where we will be on Saturday. The Youth from Stornoway are going there too. It was great to talk to Sandra. Her pastor had visited her when we arrived yesterday. We tell her about the 'Journey' and we give her a leaflet. A photo is taken, we pack our things into our car greatly encouraged.

We travel onto Inverness. It is an amazing journey, the day is warm, we travel over Skye Bridge across the mainland to Loch Ness to Inverness. The mountains are awesome, there are sheep everywhere. There is snow on the mountains, brooks babble as water flowed across them. We drive quickly as we need to get to Inverness fairly soon. We look at the mountains, the lochs, in the vastness of them,

It was as if time did not exist. You feel small in the vastness. You can understand how King David felt when he looked at the mountains, 'What is man, the Son of Man, that you have made him a little lower than the angels. Psalm 8:4-6. God is vast, even more vast than those mountains, infinite, yet He cares for you and me, He became a man, a human being in the world, He was created, a baby in His mothers womb.

Jesus also tells us how much he cares for us and His creation. There will be times when we will feel alone, He promises that He will be there for us always. King David wrote the Psalms and how He felt. The Psalms fit all our feelings. David had to flee from Saul many times living the life of a fugitive, living where ever he could with his army of men. Jesus once said of Himself, "Foxes have lairs but the Son of man has nowhere to lay His head". Both knew the pain of being homeless. Jesus was pursued by the Pharisees and the Sadducees, the religious men of His day who would one day nail Him to the Cross, while David was pursued by Saul who to was trying to kill him. Both men were kings, David was an earthly one, while Jesus is the Heavenly one.

View from Skye to Inverness

There will be times when we will feel betrayed, where people will not like us. The Bible tells us, 'Do not put your trust in Princes', Psalm 146:3 meaning man, but always put your trust in God and you cannot go wrong. Loch Ness is beautiful, it is the deepest loch in Scotland, there is a museum dedicated to Nessie the Loch Ness monster. We notice the countryside changing very much from Stornoway with no peat. We stop at a chalet type cafe for a drink where there are three German bikers, it is very pleasant. There are loads of chaffinches feeding off a tray in a tree, we have our tea and go on our way. Soon we are in Inverness that reminds us of Kingston in Surrey. It is very busy. We find the bed and breakfast, we unpack, change, we set off to the town with our banner. We look around and pray for a spot.

We find one opposite a bank and set off to have lunch. We find a Morrisons, this shop is large, like most of these supermarkets has a big restaurant where we have our meal. We go back to our spot in the High Street and put up the banner. The wind is blowing but we manage. A younger man is near us, he is selling crafts, some made by himself some by other people. He has long hair with a tartan headband, he is wearing silver earrings and a shirt with jeans. He tells us he raises money for charity by swimming across Loch Ness every year which he says is cold. He sang "Jesus, Jesus." Other men come along to help him. He comes into town every day.

The people go by looking, but not coming too near. A young woman comes nearby explaining to her friend about idols. She explains that Christians do not like statues which was interesting as being the second Commandment, 'you shall not make for yourself an idol'. Another lady comes with her daughter and takes a leaflet. She is of West Indian origin. Then two Christians come along and speak to us. They are on holiday from Aberdeen and are encouraged by what we are doing. They have been Christians for many years. They have a Brethren and Free Church background. They speak of the Country in dire need of the Word of God. They tell us about a book written by Robert Comfort on the Ten Commandments and of Christians coming out to evangelise. We pray that we have encouraged them. They tell us about the young man selling crafts. He has a Christian background. We go back to the bed and breakfast. There is a leaflet in the foyer about a cafe called the Mustard Seed which is mentioned in the Bible.

Street proclamation in Inverness centre

In our bedroom we prayed. We have a vision, we see a man on a horse dressed as a page, he has a long trumpet in his hand, along the trumpet a scroll is unfurled. He is a messenger. We realise that this is a battle of the Heavenlies, we had done our bit to sow the seed now it was over to Jesus how

He wanted the seed to grow. Jesus speaks of the mustard seed in Mark 4 :30, He explains that the mustard seed is very small yet when it grows it becomes the largest of all the garden plants.

We try to get a Christian channel on the radio but happen to tune into a satellite one, two men from South Carolina are doing Christian teaching. They preaching from the Book of Revelation and the seventh angel. They then give two telephone numbers and a free gift to let those know who heard the programme contact them. The seventh angel in the book of Revelation plays a trumpet, it is about Jesus reigning for ever and ever, and judgement.

We travelled 76 miles from Lochalsh in Skye to Inverness.

Wednesday 4 June

We are chatting to our hostess Hilary at breakfast, she tells us that she used to work as a secretary in Pall Mall, London. Hilary and her husband have made the lounge into a beautiful room. There is a glass replica of Nessie on the window sill, with a huge cabinet of glass and crystal in the corner of the room, with colours glistening in the morning light. It reminds us of many years ago when people would have glass cabinets displaying their crystal and glass ware, not many people do this now but it can be very effective. Breakfast is over we say good-bye to our hosts and leave. Soon we are on our way to John O'Groats leaving behind Inverness. We drive through countryside. There seems to be a place called Easter, we see this name twice. the land is changing, becoming more rugged. We go round hairpin roads with steep sides as it becomes more coastal with the sea below. Scotland is a land of contrasts, very beautiful. We stop at a petrol station which seems very American. The type of vehicles going past also seem American.

We go over a long bridge into John O'Groats to our next bed and breakfast where there are German and Australian flags. We are able to put our things into the bed and breakfast and change as well as having a rest after all the hairpin bends.

Jesus often walked rugged countryside and sea. There were many types of animals in Israel, sheep, goats, donkeys, hares to name but a few. Jesus spoke of a passage way which was used by travellers for taking their goods to sell but notorious for people being robbed by thieves as the passageway ran between two sets of mountains where the thieves would hide and wait for people to come through, the thieves would be armed with knives. The passageway was called the 'Bloody Way' for obvious reasons.

Jesus made a parable from this. In Luke 10 an expert in the law asked Jesus, "Who is my neighbour?", Jesus answered him telling him the story of the Good Samaritan based on this passageway. The Levite and the priest mentioned would go through this passageway. The Samaritans were considered as a half breed by the Jews. As they had inter married with other people, not Jews. They split leaving the Samaritans having to have their own temple in Samaria, they never mixed or worshipped together. Jesus goes on to tell the story of a man who was stripped, beaten and left for dead. The priest and the Levite refuse to help him but the Samaritan stopped and gave him first aid, took him to an inn and nursed him over night, he goes in and pays the money and leaves enough money for the man to be looked after, promising he will pay any extra money when he travelled through again. Jesus after telling the expert this story asked which of these three was a neighbour to the man who fell into the hand of robbers. The expert replied the one who helped him. Jesus told him to do the same.

It is hard in life to help people today as then, we have violent crime and theft, but we must never lose our compassion to help people. People need the Gospel, it is not enough helping our families and those who are our friends, the Gospel is for everyone. That someone could be someone's grandchild, daughter, son. Someone may be praying for them wondering where they are. Jesus commands us, "Love your neighbour as yourself". We are the family of God, Jesus commands us to go out to the world and give the Good News, how the whole company of Heaven will rejoice when a person is saved. It is not easy when the person does not like you or they are not the sort of person you associate with, show mercy when you can, the Samaritans were disliked but Jesus used a Samaritan in His story to show that he helped a person who probably hated him because of who he was. The Levite and priests were Jews but they did not help their fellow man.

We travel to John O'Groats, it is not far from the guest house. We pass the Castle of Mey, the late Queen Mother's home. John O' Groats has a small square with shops and crafts, there a signpost with John O'Groats written on it for photographs, tourists pay for this. We pray about where to stand then we have a meal in the cafeteria and have a look around. We go to John O'Groats house where there is a museum. The museum tells us the history of 1918 when the German boats surrendered to the British. The battalion of boats is massive. You begin to realise what Winston Churchill did. It becomes more real than history, the war being won. The newspaper cuttings bring it to life of what actually happened at that time.

We leave the museum and set up our banner and wait. People go backwards and forwards. No-one comes up to speak, it feels strange. An attendant gets alarmed as we are in front of the shopping parade. Loads of tourists pass reading the banner, they are of all nationalities., We have a lovely view of the sea and stay for an hour. We fold up the banner and go back to the bed and breakfast where we find a Gidion Bible which we use.

We are reminded of the beginning of John's beautiful Gospel, 'In the beginning was the Word. and the Word was Light. The Light came into the world but the world comprehended it not.'

Sometimes standing with the banner the world seems indifferent, it passes by. The world thinks little about Jesus but it is more concerned with its cares. If only the world would cast its cares to the one who made the world, the creator who hung on the Cross as the world passed Him by just as it does today. Jesus gave the parable of the sower sowing seeds, John the Apostle spoke of us who are in Christ being the Light of the World who need to take the seed of that Word and let it shine as a light in our hearts.

We travel 120 miles from Inverness to John O'Groats

44

Thursday 5 June

Today we set off for Orkney, we are up early. John our host was up early and very kindly made us breakfast. The day is starting to get very warm we set off for the ferry from Scrabster to Stromness. We arrive and go onto the ferry that is a two hour crossing. We park our car in the hull and go upstairs into the lounge. We look round and we see on the television an interview with Tony Blair. The reception is not that good. He is talking about Israel and Palestine, that Palestine needs her own land. He went on to talk about his own family, the programme showed us how hard it is to be a Prime Minister and how difficult it is to be with your family at that time. It is not an easy job for who ever leads their party and government, there has to be a balance between the party and family.

Ferry crossing from Scrabster to Stromness, Orkneys

The journey is smooth. We sit on the open deck enjoying the day, then we go for a drink downstairs. We chat to a ferry server who has been in many jobs to do with the sea and other countries including Saudi Arabia and Glasgow, although deep down he is Orkney bred and born. He loves his Island as do many people.

We go upstairs and the view coming into port was breath taking with the green hills and houses coming into view with a lovely sunshine. We go to our car and drive onto land. The land is very green, there are many sheep, cows and horses. We have not seen many cows and horses until now. We stop for petrol, we see notices for Christian healing by Christian prayer in the local Church, it is so wonderful to see this. We drive on amidst the golden and yellow colours of flowers adorning the roadside like miniature versions of sunlight. We arrive at Kirkwall the principal town that is a twenty miles from the ferry and it is beautiful, we even see a golden sheep. We drive fast. We stop at a museum mill for a break where there is a shop with books, handmade jewellery which is beautifully created.

We arrive at the bed and breakfast in good time, we have a break and set forth. We walk to the town which is a lovely walk in the sunshine. We arrive and pray looking round the town to find a spot for our banner which is near an ice cream shop. We go for lunch, after lunch we set up the banner, it is an interesting afternoon. There seem to be a lot of young people around, they are aged from twelve years of age upwards. They pass with comments with one young man saying he did not believe in Jesus. We find that young people are very honest in what they believe and come straight out with what they think. They come backwards and forwards very interested. Three young men come up, "Your wearing a hat, are you Australian", one asked. We responded "No". "When was Jesus born?" another asked, "How old was He when He died on the Cross?" "How old was He when He rose from the grave.?" they asked. Young people are very perceptive and they are clear in their asking. There is such a spiritual hunger. Once the disciples would not let the children come to Jesus. He told the disciples, "Let them come unto me. Unless you are as one of these you will never enter the Kingdom of God." Mark 10 :13.

Kirkwall quayside, principal town of the Orkneys

The young are crying out for God today. They need us to tell them about Jesus. They have questions to ask. We are now having generations of people whose parents are drug takers, alcoholics, promiscuous, we need to break the chains that they are free in Jesus. We have seen young people as young as ten years of age riding round late at night. Fifteen year olds sniffing glue yet the message of Christ is not reaching them. We as Christians are responsible, yes for our own children, grandchildren, nieces, nephews and relatives but Jesus wants us to share our faith with everyone. Most people come to faith through another Christian sharing their faith. One of our fathers became a Christian on his deathbed through two Christians who were neighbours in his street, always telling him that Jesus loved Him and others praying for him as he lay dying.

These young people need us to tell them about Jesus, who else is going to do it, they may have no-one in the family to tell them so we can become spiritual parents and pray for them. Life for them is not easy, it can be tough for them.

The afternoon went on. Colin popped into the ice cream parlour. A man from Norway stopped him. "I know you, I have seen you in Inverness." How exciting. Madeleine has a break from holding the banner. A man comes along and speaks to Madeleine. It is difficult at first to understand what he is saying as his Scottish is broad but he explained that he was a photographer from the local paper. He takes a photo and leaves, We are amazed and pleased. At 5 o'clock we fold up the banner and go. We walk back to the bed and breakfast, we pass a family in their garden having a barbecue while their two dogs have a good bark at us. In the bed and breakfast we have a view of the sea. A fog descends, the lights twinkle in the foggy darkness.

We are again reminded of John's Gospel, "The Light came into the darkness, but the light comprehended it not." No-matter what we go through in life, however dark it may seem like the lights shining in the fog. The Light of Christ will shine through.

In the trials of these young people they can still be reached in the fog of rejection. Christ can be their Light. We can give them that hope that Christ will be their anchor for life. What a privilege to give these young ones hope with a healthier, moral, cleaner life, free from drugs, free from drink, free from violence. Amen.

We travel 37 miles from John O'Groats to Kirkwall, Orkneys. This included 17 miles travelling by Ferry from Scrabster to Stromness.

Friday 6 June

We were up early to get to the ferry at 4.00 am. We have cereal, tea, we sit in the lounge for a while then we drive off. We arrive at the ferry, we go to the ticket office then we pass through and wait. Near us in the queue are two vans for horses, they decide to have a sortie just as the ferry is taking us on board. A man shouts to them to get a move on, they quickly finish. We drive onto the ferry and go upstairs. Many people are tired, the Captain and Skipper greet us over the intercom, we fall asleep. Later on we have refreshments, soon it is time to leave the ferry. We drive off into thick fog which is on the road bend. A lorry is in front of us, the driver is driving very carefully, the name on his van is Gordon & Mcphain and we are driving behind him a long time until he allows us to pass. We pray for God to remove the fog. A small wind appears and drives the fog away. We are pleased with this answer to prayer. we pass a pottery and mould. We travel from the Orkneys to Aberdeen moving swiftly to get there on time. There is another place called Easter. The name reminds us of Easter, the Resurrection of Jesus and His victory over death. We pass a Free Range farm, the chickens look very healthy. A man sits on some steps in the middle of them, it is so nice to see the animals and man are such friends. There are also more cows this way, horses and ponies. We come into Aberdeen, it is a huge industrial city. Aberdeen was once a fishing Port but had grown with the railway boom, there are many stone buildings alongside the Victorian ones, we find our bed and breakfast, we have an upstairs view from our window. We can see from our window modern houses opposite with a hill road with an iron bridge with the Tudor rose upon it. There are stone houses at the top of the hill with an extra storey put on top, they have no front gardens, the doors go straight onto the street. The Victorian houses have front doors and railings which look originals, in London many railings were taken down for the war effort, many from parks which were never replaced. We have a rest then set off for Aberdeen centre.

We walk towards the city centre and ask a bicycle shop for directions to the town, they tell us where to go. We realise as we come out of the shop we have forgotten the banner so the banner is duly collected. We move swiftly into town. We pray for God's help to show us where to put the banner. In the Centre our names are called, a lady from Stornoway recognises us. She works in Mckinnons the bakery next door to The Father's House, we have a chat explaining what we are doing. We then say good-bye to her also her husband and daughter. There are many people in the City so it was amazing to meet her. We find a spot and we leave to have a meal. We go back to our spot, the local Primark shop which has a brick wall space where we will not interfere with the shoppers or trip the shoppers up with our banner. Two women come and take leaflets quietly, they go. It is an interesting afternoon, the City is busy. Opposite us on the other side of the road is a side road going downhill, people looked very small and as they came uphill looked bigger, while you hold the banner looking down the high street to the right, there too is a hill. As we hold the banner It feels as if you are on the Cross looking down, people passing indifferent, carrying on their way as though the banner was not there. "As it was in the days of Noah, so it will be at the coming of the Son of Man", Jesus said. People will carry on as normal living their lives, Jesus explains, just as the floods came in Noah's time when Noah entered the ark and swept the people away because they would not listen to Noah about the flood coming because of their wickedness, so the Son of Man will come like a flood, sweeping over us as we still do not listen to what God is telling us that He is coming back one day, we continue living our life our own ways. Matthew 24 :36.

At the scene of the crucifixion, the disciples watched. The Romans carried on as usual, another man dying, they play for his clothes at the foot of the Cross. You can feel His tears come down. His love for His people asking them to come back. His Love for them as He said upon the Cross, "Forgive them Father for they know not what they do." As we think about Moses in a battle against a tribe called Amalekites he had to hold up his hands, when he grew tired his hands came down, the battle went the enemies way. When he kept his arms up Israel was winning. Two men, Aaron, Moses brother, and Hur came forward and helped Moses keep up his arms on each side, they won the battle against the Amalekites. This represented Jesus on the Cross who was victorious.

We finish at 6.50pm, we pray and go back to the bed and breakfast. This poem came to us.

Remember me, I died on the cross at Calvary. You pass me by, you cry give me proof. I died in agony and pain so that sin in your life will not reign. I gave you the Bible, the Word so that My voice will again be heard, remember Me who died in agony, you will once again see, the man who died upon the Cross, for mankind's victory, the devil's loss.

At the bed and breakfast we find a brief history of Ballater, the area where we are staying, in a church magazine and also a Gideon's Bible. Ballatar was a scattering of houses when a lady named Elspet Michie who was suffering form scrofula (Inflammation of the lymph glands) discovered the restorative powers of the spring waters at Pannanick Wells. The village was to change and grow. Ballater also had the railway boom. In 1800 it had its own church, its first service 14 December 1800. A man called Frances Farquhanson made the water more known and many people came for healing. Before the waters were made known the ecclesiastical civic centre had been a place called Tullick. It is now Glenuich (Ballater) Parish Church, Church of Scotland.

Jesus Gospels too are full of healings, when John the Baptist was thrown into prison he wanted to make sure that Jesus was who He said He was. John sent his disciples round to see Jesus. "Tell John," Jesus replied, "The blind see, the lame walk, those who have leprosy are cured, the deaf hear, the dead are raised, the Good News is preached to the poor. Luke 7:20-22. The sign of the Messiah coming was healing. We too can trust in the Man from Galilee. He can heal the lame, the broken hearted. Pray for your loved ones today because prayer can move mountains. Jesus loves beyond measure, He loves us all and wants us back. He never forces his way in but waits at the door of our hearts asking us if He can come in. What a great God we have if only we would open that door and let Him in.

We travelled 258 miles from Kirkwall, Orkneys to Aberdeen City.

We leave Aberdeen, and say good-bye to Hilary and Sandy and set forth for Edinburgh, as we go into the street we see baby seagulls on a roof. We leave early, the day is hot as we drive along, the countryside is looking more and more like England with the beautiful colours of summer, gold purple, white flowers adorning the country side making it so colourful. Many sheep now have been clipped. They look so different, sadly we pass a baby deer killed by traffic alongside other casualties. There have also been sightings of bunnies moving along the verges. We come into Edinburgh amidst the fields of sheep, cows and a piggery. We have not seen a piggery for years. We see a beautiful Golden Eagle sitting on a post. We have tried to use our sat-nav but the voice has vanished so we have to work our own way out of the city which proves difficult. The AA map is at hand. The sat-nav stays silent, we stop at a cafe and post a letter. There is a shop which has Scottish souvenirs, the ladies are Scottish and they are listening to Radio 2. The mobile phone rings informing us that a relative has just died. We pray for our family. We then drive on.

We arrive in Edinburgh and ask a postman the way to our bed and breakfast, we find it and are welcomed by our hosts Neal and Lesley. We put our things in our room, freshen up and decide to walk to the town, we take our hats, but in the end realise that we need to catch a bus with our things as they are heavy. As usual people are very friendly and helpful. We arrive in Edinburgh which is an amazing lively city. We walk round and see John Knox's house, he was an ardent Scottish Protestant and had determination to stop the Catholic Mary Queen of Scots having the Scottish throne. She was forced off the throne by the Scottish parliament in 1567 after succeeding the throne from her mother Mary of Guise who died in 1560. In 1560 the Scottish parliament passed laws after Mary of Guise died which stopped the Pope having any say in any of the religious affairs on how Scotland was run and no one was to celebrate Mass as it was made illegal. Mary Queen of Scots had been living in France, she came back to Scotland a year later in 1561 after her mother Mary of Guise had died where she celebrated Mass in Edinburgh, she had broken the new laws made by the Scottish parliament, John Knox's preaching and the government ruling, her son James VI of Scotland and the future James 1 of England who was bought up by Protestant guardians. His mother, an ardent Catholic, was not allowed to be near him. Mary tried to get the throne of England instead but she never succeeded in this quest as she was taken prisoner by Queen Elizabeth 1 and her government and executed.

After we have a look around and pray for our spot we go to the Robbie Burns restaurant, the poet of Scotland,. This man was a Scottish farmer and poet. Every year people celebrate Burns night with haggis that is a Scottish dish and Robbie's poems. As we eat we look out of the window and see opposite us a Christmas shop open, a new age shop advertising Tarot readings, in the restaurant where we are eating a poster too is advertising Tarot readings. By our table on the window sill are the Jewish candles of seven, we realise what a hotch potch of beliefs are around and how much man needs God. We finish our meal and go into the square opposite. The Fringe Theatre shop is here and on the yard there are plays. The Fringe does comedy and plays, every year there is the Edinburgh Festival, the City is alive with many things happening in the Arts.

We set up our banner, a young Chinese couple are selling scarves and jewellery, they are very friendly, a tame pigeon joins us, he sits with us all quite content in front of the banner, there is a comedy inacted in front of us with a crowd of people. People are going round dressed in costumes. There are women walking round with veils and tiaras. A group of Hawaiian dancers and a woman in a pink medieval costume. The afternoon is hot. Down the road is a hugh church steeple to our left.

Several people take leaflets, we are blessed by the visit of two Assembly of God Pentecostal ministers of the area who knew Donnie and Catriona from Stornoway. After they leave two men come up and give their testimonies. They are in their early forties and gave their lives to the Lord about ten years ago when both were alcoholics, one admitted that it was hard to keep off the drink but Jesus gives him the faith to go on.

A Horse Guard Calvary man who had worked in London comes to speak, he asks many questions including about the Toronto blessing. He is in his early forties, he goes to the Church of Scotland. We next meet a man and his lady companion, he has been in Saudi Arabia where he had been speaking with the Muslims about the Koran, he was asking Christians about Christianity, while he chatted another young man comes and joins in, then the other man and his companion leave. The young man asks many questions. While we were chatting a man dressed as an angel in black and grey from head to foot with black wings goes past, it looks very strange.

While the young man spoke we have a vision, we look down the street at the high tower, we see Jesus, He is as high as the tower, He is massive, He holds out His hands. In His right hand are sheep which He holds carefully and in His left hand are goats, they are falling out of His hands.

The afternoon has been good, we pack away our banner and go. It has been a great day. It is wonderful to hear these testimonies and enquiries, it is greatly encouraging. We see many nationalities, the place is a throng of people. We take a bus back to the bed and breakfast.

When we look at the events of the afternoon we are reminded of the parable of the sower, we must pray for the seed to stay in men's hearts and minds and pray that many will come to know God.

We travelled 126 miles from Aberdeen to Edinburgh.

Sunday 8 June

It is our last day in Scotland, we say good-bye to Lesley and Neal, we set off for Glasgow. It is a beautiful day, the countryside is colourful with sheep, cattle and horses. It is very quiet everywhere being a Sunday. The drive is easy going, we see brown sheep and another place called Easter. We see pyramids near plateau's, hills of colours and plush farmland which is like green velvet. We take a break at a place called Wild Beans. We arrive in Glasgow where we are welcomed at the bed and breakfast. There is a mixture of cultures here like London, many people are of an Asian descent. We are welcomed by John and Tony. The people living in these roads have a broad Scottish accent. We refresh ourselves and then decide to walk to the town, we see a road called John Knox, as we walk along we see statutes of William Gladstone who was Prime Minister four times during Queen Victoria's reign in England and Robert Peel founder of the police force. His men were called Peelers and also Red Robins after their red coats and bobbies after the name of Robert. We also see a piece about the 1688 Glorious Revolution which is about freedom and liberty. James II succeeded his brother Charles 11 on the throne of England, James unwisely decided to make make the country Catholic, he made himself vastly unpopular, when his son was born there were fears that he would be brought up as a Catholic. James had a daughter Mary who was married to William of Orange, William a Protestant was invited by Protestant statesmen to have the English throne. William agreed to this, he landed at Torbay and marched to London, James II fled to France and William along with his wife Mary were offered the throne to rule jointly which they agreed to do.

Edinburgh centre

We see pipers and bands of all colours and hue, there are men and women of all ages as we walk through. The day is hot but it is too far to walk to Glasgow so we finish the walk by bus. We alight from the bus, we pray while we walk through the city and find a spot for the banner. We ask two council workers for a place to eat, they direct us. The meal is superb. As we come out of the cafe the city is alive, full of people. While we set up the banner a piper plays the hymn, 'The day Thou Gavest, Now has Ended.' It was nice to start the afternoon with this tune. We are opposite a tea place. On our right hand side is a stall run by the British Red Cross in aid of the Chinese earthquake with young dancers aged from 6 to teenage. Further along is a tent covering for Muslims chatting to others about their faith.

The Chinese girls of all ages do dancing to raise money. The younger girls have colourful dresses of orange, yellows, red, blue, white. They have red socks with colourful aprons with yellow sashes, Yellow aprons with squares, their dark hair plaited. the older girls wear hats, black mid rib cardigans and green trousers with red patterns with shoes. The young women dance very well with people filming them. The males came along later carrying Red Cross buckets. People look at the banner but do not speak, although leaflets are taken. We pray for people to be touched, as the crowd thins out we let down our banner and take a taxi home.

The houses around the bed and breakfast are Victorian, they are huge. Tony is the receptionist, his family own bed and breakfasts around the area. He brought this bed and breakfast which needed renovating. The house has been beautifully restored, the shower here is unusual, it has a Jacuzzi with water spraying from all angles as well as a normal shower and built in radio. Tony also likes football.

We meet a man from Canada who is of Scottish descent with a Scottish name, he has come to Glasgow to live. He tells us that there are similarities in Scotland and Canada, he is very happy.

We are reminded again as we think of the day, in Matthew 25:31, the sheep and the goats for the vision we had of Christ, that Jesus will come back to the earth and sit on his throne judging the nations, with the sheep on his left and the goats on His right. He will bless the sheep on his right and send the goats into the eternal hell fire destined for the devil and his angels. As to the recent Chinese earthquake we can look in Matthew 24:1-8 explaining about signs of the end of the age. In Matthew 28 we are commissioned to tell people the Good News, Jesus tells His disciples before He ascends to Heaven to go and make disciples of all nations. It is a command of joy for us to go out and give the Good News to people in the highways and byways. At that time Jesus had risen but some of the disciples still doubted but Jesus has told them He was with them even to the end of the age. Matthew 28:18.

We can be bold if we obey the Holy Spirit as He instructs and leads us. Sometimes it is small things. Jesus may tell us to go to a certain place, we do not know why, we go to the person He has sent and they are saved. We are living in a world where there is little faith in Christ yet we are called to be a witness of faith. Yes we have faith and yes we are saved but we have the command to go out and tell others about Jesus. When a child is born we do not keep it to ourselves, no, we want to tell everyone of this gift of a child that has been given. Is it the same with Jesus, when we have received Him in our lives, we have a faith, a wonderful faith that is a gift from Him that can be shared with others. we should not keep it to ourselves, this wonderful news of Christ, a gift to the world, our world . Amen

We travelled 46 miles from Edinburgh to Glasgow.

Northern Ireland

Monday 9 June

We are up early, John very kindly makes us breakfast. He has been doing the night reception. He was born and brought up in Glasgow and is very happy here. He makes us very welcome, we have a lovely chat then we say farewell to John and Glasgow. We drive to Stranraer Ferry to cross over to Belfast. We travel down winding roads, there is a field lush with grass with water being sprayed. the land is so wonderfully green. There are road works with red beacons, like solders all in a line telling you where not to drive, one has to be careful as we go towards the ferry port, there is a hugh rock in the sea which seems to go alongside us, the fresh smell of the sea comes into the car. As we go to turn down another winding road there is a rock on our right which has the words painted 'Jesus died for us' which really encourages us. We go down to the Ferry and security is tight. People's cars are being checked, we go to the car park. The police come round to check. To freshen up or eat in the restaurant you have to go through a little reception room, take a card, go to the restaurant, come back and give the card back before you return to the car. We get lost with the arrows telling you where to go, it is no good being in a hurry, you can get lost. We manage to get some sandwiches.

Ferry crossing from Stranraer to Belfast

We at last go onto the ferry, it is very different from the other ferries as you go up silver slopes in your car, you have a deck number and colour. You leave the car and go onto deck. The ferry is huge. The Captain welcomes us and his mate give out safety instructions, which in their strong accents was difficult to understand what they are saying. Fortunately there is a visual television which you can see and read. The ship starts to move, we are off, we are enjoying the journey, we are feeling very sleepy. We read newspapers and magazines, the journey is smooth, the seagulls fly around us, the rock that is situated just off the coast can still be seen as we sail. There are two restaurants, one which is at a higher level than where we are sitting, one on our level. We meet a lady called Ann, she tells people that she has come to Ireland to see her Mammy. She comes from Glasgow. Towards the end of our journey we move to the front and see Ireland come into view. We take a picture, all too soon the tranny asks us to go to our cars, which we do. Unfortunately the sat nav is affected and the sound is faint.

The greenery is like Scotland, the colours of Summer are ablaze. You can also see England in this beauty. It is a nice drive. As we approach Derry we see a building advertising a 'Christian Gospel Drive In'. We also see a poster advertising 'Healing the Land.' A man is coming from South Africa to preach which is encouraging. As we came nearer to Derry we see plateau's which looked like hills that have had a knife sliced across them making them flat. We pass a lady hymn writers house. Here too are timber trees that are different from Scotland.

We find the bed and breakfast with the aid of an AA map, we ask people who are very helpful with their dog and child walking. The bed and breakfast is near a college so there are many young people here, when we are ready, we go out with our banner. We pray as usual but for some reason we feel uneasy. We pass a gate where James II of England was not allowed into the city and then ensued a huge battle named 'Battle of the Boyne. James II at this time had lost his throne, William of Orange marched up to Ireland, there was the first battle, known as the the Battle of the Boyne, a second battle came 'Battle of Aughrim', both battles were lost by James 11. After this battle James II effectively finished the line of the Stuarts as Kings of England. We are reminded of the 'Battle of the Boyne' as each year on July 12 the Orangemen remember this event in history.

We decide to go and see Brian the manager at the Faith Mission Bookshop, we feel we need the seed of prayer. A taxi driver takes us to the shop, he finds the shop for us, we meet Brian and have a wonderful prayer time. We have a vision of Satan falling like lighting. We decide to do the banner in the morning. We feel it is right to get advice from someone who knows the area. We go back to the bed and breakfast, the church bells are ringing . They play to our astonishment ' The day Thou gavest has ended,' just as the piper had played two days ago in Scotland.

Following God's call is not always easy. Moses thought himself a weak speaker. God sent Moses brother Aaron to help him, gradually Moses took over, Aaron eventually did the ministry he was given which was to be a priest, as did their sister Miriam who was a prophetess and dancer. We can do things if God wants us to do something, He can carry it through with us as He did with Moses, for whatever He has asks us to do things for Him we only have to do as He asks and He will do the rest. Jesus said, "I have come to do the will of He who sent me." If Jesus can do God's will then so can we. Amen.

Outside Christian Bookshop in Derry

We travelled 86 miles from Glasgow to Stranraer Ferry , 60 miles across the Ferry to Belfast and 70 from Belfast to Derry.

Tuesday 10 June

Today we walk past the college, the college has a Latin name which we translated as Light of Christ. There is a symbol of a dove with her 'olive branch'. This too is a name of a project which we run. Many years ago we were sitting as a group of people looking for a name for the project we were starting, the Lord gave us the passage from Noah about the Olive Branch. No-one was sure about this name so it was left for a few weeks then we knew that this was the name God had given, it is a lovely symbol for friendship. If we fall out with someone we can offer them an 'olive branch', the hand of friendship, telling them that we are sorry for what we have done. It is very overcast today, we have left our luggage in the bed and breakfast, we walk into the town, we put

57

up the banner opposite the memorial in the town, it is very cold. The wind is blowing hard. We are near a bus stop, we are standing in front of two phone boxes on the pavement, across the way there is a Yoga Healing Centre. The town begins to fill with people, there is a family department store which has a tea shop, the store is the first department store we have seen in N Ireland, it is a little like Tiffanys in London. The War Memorial is interesting. An angel stands on top holding a laurel wreath in the right hand victorious, the angel's left foot is crushing a snake round its neck, below is a statue of a naval man and a soldier, this commemorates the Second World War.

This reminded us of the book of Genesis when Satan in the guise of a snake came into the garden and tempted Eve with the apple which she ate. Eve and Adam fell. The beautiful garden tainted by sin. God punished Adam and Eve, an animal created by God was killed to clothe Adam and Eve who were both naked. The snake was condemned to crawl without legs, so the World was left in a sorry state. In Genesis we are told that the snake's head would be crushed by a child of our first parents, this child was to be Jesus who defeated Satan on the Cross. Sadly the first record of murder of a man was Adam and Eve's son Cain who murdered his brother Abel. Today man still rebels, he does his own thing, we do as we feel, we have, we want, we get. In marriage if our spouse does not suit then we go onto the next one. We want children when we want them, we want to be a single parent, others decide that they do not want to be a dad after all and leaves mum doing the job of two, wouldn't it be better to put our faith in God who will bring us the right person if we pray. He may not desire us to marry or have children as He can use us all in His work to pray for others and for others to come to know Him. We can pray for our family to know our Lord but as Jesus pointed out, who is my mother, brother. Those who obey the will of my Father. He loved His earthly parents and family but there is a spiritual one too as He pointed out. His family is whoever does the will of His Father. Matthew 12:46-49.

We notice many acorn trees and indeed there was a young one where we stood, a chaffinch wings its way in and out. Engraved on the ground and on the chairs are acorns and acorn leaves everywhere.

People look at the banner from afar. No-one stops to speak. So we pray for them. There are cobbled stones near our feet, these are from the days when they were put in place for women to cross the road as their skirts were long and could get quite dirty.

We fold up our banner and walk back to the bed and breakfast. We pass a law court, we collect our bags and say "good bye" to Catherine our host. We sit in the lounge for a few minutes. There is a Bible by the television. We pack our things into the car and travel back to Brian and the Christian Bookshop. We have a photo taken with Brian outside the shop, it has been great meeting him, we say 'good-bye' and set off for Donegal. The scenery is as in Scotland, breathtaking, there are lots of trees and tree felling. We are reminded of the trees in Scotland whose cones looked like candles coming up from the trees.

We see water flowing over the brooks, it is very poetical.

The story of Moses comes to mind. As he is tending his sheep the fire of God consumes the bush, Moses goes forward wondering what is going on. Yahweh speaks to him. Moses is commissioned to go forward to set the people free. From this commission Moses went, he freed the Hebrews from the Egyptians, they become the nation of Israel. Exodus 3.

We see many posters for the Euro vote, for and against. We listen to the news, they are saying that the votes seem to be neck and neck. We have lost the bed and breakfast and we end up in someone's forecourt, a dog comes out, we decide to stay in the car realising that it is not the bed and breakfast. We drive out quickly, further down the road we find a care home where a carer gives us directions.

We find our bed and breakfast which is on a farm. The views are amazing, we unpack and we go and have a look round Donegal which is a nice town. We see a truck of sheep in a small cart baaing together as they go round. Donegal is a medium size town, there are some great walks, it is well worth the visit for the excellent scenery and like Scotland, Ireland has lovely home-made food.

Donegal Morrows, the man who previously owned the bed and breakfast was a descendent of a chieftain who owned the castle. The bed and breakfast is very much into recycling. A green bin for old bits, a blue one for plastics, paper etc. There are churches near by and there is a list on the reception about the different churches and times. We can hear in our room the baaing of sheep which is nice.

This too brings to mind of Jesus our Shepherd, each sheep in Israel has a name. The shepherd knows them, when they move out of line he gently pulls them in with his staff. When we find Jesus we are born again. Yahweh says "Fear not for I have redeemed you, you are mine. I have called you by name." Isaac 43 verse 1

What a wonderful promise, Jesus knows us as a shepherd knows his sheep. Wow.

We travelled 46 miles from Londonderry to Donegal Town, Ireland.

Wednesday 11 June

We have breakfast to music from the era of the thirties and forties, in crooning style it is very relaxing, the singers seem to be Bing Crosby and Dean Martin. Stormy weather is one of the tunes. 'When you walk through a Storm' has been playing. This was written by Rogers and Hammerstein, this song was sang in two musical films, one by Mario Lanzo in the Student Prince, the second by Shirley Jones who was only twenty two at the time, she has a beautiful voice, she was to star years later in the Partridge Family with David Cassidy an American television serial, alongside her co-star Gordon McGrae in Carousel. Gordon McGrae was a Christian who sang alongside Jo Stafford who is a Christian too, they would sing gospel songs around America and tell people about Jesus. When Gordon died Jo carried on this work. This music is well known in football grounds in England being made popular by Gerry and the Pacemakers, many football fans sing this at football matches and occasionally by Christians. The song speaks of walking with God whatever happens in your life keep on going through all the trials and tribulations. God will get you there in the end. Walk on with hope in your heart. Add to that faith in Jesus. It is interesting to note that in Carousel, Billy, played by Gordon McGrae, who marries Laurie, played by Shirley Jones, is living a bad life, he is knifed and dies, it sounds familiar 'does it not' in today's world. Laurie goes through widowhood and she sings this song in the film.

Sometimes life does not go the way we want it, for sin has come into the world. We have to sometimes accept life for what it is. It is very hard. The exams we wanted and cannot get, the job we set our heart on and can never have, the longing for a child who never comes, the husband/wife we would love to marry but we remain single, we would love a brother, sister but we remain an only child, the list goes on.... .

We have a Father who understands, a God who has been here in human form as Jesus conceived by the Holy Spirit. His earthly dad Joseph, who looked after Him, died. Jesus wept in the garden of Gethsemane, He was ridiculed and called names because the Pharisees thought His mother had conceived Jesus by another man. The Pharisees even went so far to say that Jesus was half a Samaritan as Samaritans were hated by the Jews as they had married outside the Jewish race, which indeed he was not. On the Cross He was reviled with many people against Him. He asked John to look after his mother Mary while He was dying on the cross. He cried for His friend Lazaurus whom He raised from the dead. He prayed, taught about his Father, He did healing. He continued in faith with His Father even unto the Cross. He never stopped taking about Him and neither should we for He loves us with an everlasting Love. As Jesus suffered on the Cross, He held onto His Father and so should we. The Psalms are full of people holding onto their faith in God.

We say good-bye to our hosts, the Morrows, we set forth for Amargh. We see some sheep, they are very coffee coloured. The sat-nav goes quiet and we are lost. The road seems to go two ways. We go onto the roundabout, we go round three times and pick the wrong road. We end up by a church which has a shrine of the Virgin Mary and a statue of Bernadette in the grass. There is a firm next door to the church so we go there and ask for directions. We have gone completely the wrong way so we go back to where we started. We travel along a really hilly road with bumps within bumps. It is a bit like a fairground ride. We stop in a small village not knowing where to go as there are no name signs or road posts. We stop outside a place called the Diamond Bar, in front of us is a War Memorial to World War Two, to our right is a newsagent with tables outside set with second hand bits and pieces with a young lady sales assistant with her mobile. We are astonished to see above the Diamond bar signs the words Merry Christmas and Santa on his ladder ready to be on the move. One supposes as Christmas comes earlier and earlier each year it is quicker to leave your lights on the wall.

We decide to go up a road and find directions. We find a car place, they give us directions. We see a name on the road Ferigadal. We travel on with the sat nav in my hand listening, it felt like holding an old fashioned hearing aid. We travel on passing some giant gnomes in a garden, we pass through Omagh to Armagh. We find a house for the bed and breakfast, there is a dog in the garden just like before, we stay in our seats just in case it is not the bed and breakfast, the owner comes out and confirms that it is. A cat nestles under a tree. We check in, refresh ourselves and set off for Amargh. We noticed when we were in Ireland that the signs are in kilometres not in miles as in England. We are working in three currencies, Irish, English and Euro. Sometimes we are given Euro money which some shops accept with great enthusiasm while some do not, they tell you how much cheaper your goods are in Euro and what a bargain. If only you can understand what the bargain is in the first place, it makes life very interesting.

We park and set forth, we have lunch in a restaurant called Fat Sam, the lady cannot understand our English dialect nor we hers Irish but we manage. There are pictures of Humphrey Bogart and Ingrid Bergman from the film Casablanca, James Dean and Laurel and Hardy are the other pictures. After lunch we decide to visit a Christian bookshop we had seen on the way in which is also owned by 'Faith Missions', the same people as Brian's Christian shop in Derry. We meet a man called Glen and ask him to pray for us and we pray for him. Glen gives us a book on Irish history to help us understand the history of N Ireland better. We go forth to place our banner.

There is a Cathedral here, we pass a church on the way in, they are doing an ALPHA Course with another project for ladies. People see the banner and comment on it to each other but they do not come over, it is a cold day. After an hour we leave. One of our set of parents were confirmed during the war by the Bishop of Amargh, as one of our parents was in the army in World War Two, he was stationed in N Ireland, he asked if his wife could come and this was allowed and they spent three happy years here. In March 2008, Her Majesty The Queen came to Armagh to celebrate the Royal Maundy Service. Armagh that was given city status in 1995 by the Queen.

We come home and rest. We have a view of a golf driving range beside which is a field of cows busy chewing. We see what we think are butterflies, flowers flying through the air, there are golf balls. The flowers are shed where the golfers hit the balls, there are markers on the green telling you how far you have hit the ball, a black net is on the net to stop the balls flying over. A tractor has been made into a ball picker upper. It has three rollers in front with crates as baskets, as the tractor goes round the balls are scooped up by the rollers into the crates. When they are not in use they are taken off the tractor. I pop downstairs, there are people watching television in the lounge, there is an item about the Lisbon Treaty urging people to vote.

Armagh High Street

We continue our view outside our bedroom window and watching the cows chewing, the birds fly round them and underneath them pick up the pieces of food. This reminds us of the story of a Syro-Phoenician lady who comes to Jesus asking for her sick daughter to be healed. Jesus was born as a Jew, He was telling the Jews that He was God, the promised Messiah. Later after He died on the Cross His ministry would go to the Gentiles, the non Jews, through Peter who was to baptise a centurions household. Then the Good News was passed to the nations by the Apostles. This Syro-Phoenician lady realised Jesus was the Messiah, a fact that a lot of the Jews would not accept, she knew too that her daughter would be healed. She knelt at Jesus' feet asking Him to help her. Jesus tells her "It is not right to take the Children's bread and toss it to their dogs." "Yes Lord," she said "but even the dogs eat the crumbs that fall from their masters table." This may sound strange to us, but in those days people had meals with their dogs under their table, the dogs would wait for tasty tit bits. This is what Jesus and the lady were referring to. Jesus was impressed by the lady's faith. In Matthew 15 :28 we are told, "Woman you have great faith," the lady's daughter was healed. Mark 7:24 -30 also tells us this story.

If you have faith as a mustard seed it will grow, hold onto your faith, don't let go and you will find your way with joy. Mark 4:30.

We travelled 66 miles to Armagh from Donegal Town.

Today is a more restful day, we are staying two nights so we do not need to put our luggage in the car. The view from the lounge is panoramic, there are fields of cows around us, the countryside is beautiful with the clouds rolling across the sky, it is very restful.

After this we drive to Newry. We pass beautiful country, we change our car tyre at a garage as it is getting soft. We leave the sat-nav off. We reach Newry where there is a car park and canal. There are Sein Fein posters in this area. The area is a mixture of people slightly different from yesterday. We buy ourselves a salad. Then we pray and look round the area. We find a place outside Woolworths in a square. To our right is a raised square green area with two telephone boxes on top, there is a cathedral to our left, with shops across the road. We are standing next to a butchers, the smell of meat is strong especially to us as we are vegetarians. Sadly in the square there is a plaque to two men who died, shot by the British Army. There is a sculptured statue portraying Newry history to 1194, from where where we are standing we can see a boat with a sail with a cross on it and three figures in a tower.

Newry Cathedral

The day is sunny and bright. We notice here that the young ladies from school are wearing Irish tartan of grey long skirts, it looks elegant. It is certainly different from the shorter version of the other areas. A younger school girl wears a red blazer with matching headgear and socks. People pop in and out of Woolworths buying sweets. A man comes round to look at the front of the shop, as it needs doing, he is working round the back of Woolworths and chats to a lady sitting on the wall. We chat to a family of two ladies and two small girls who have recorders, Colin shows them his harmonica. A nun goes by in a brown habit, she goes to do her shopping.

After an hour we roll up the banner. We go into the Cathedral as it is open for prayer to find out if it is Protestant or Catholic, it is Catholic, we see a group of people go across the Zebra Crossing outside the Cathedral, they come back, a gentleman crosses himself while crossing and looks at us. The zebra crossing leads to a Parish Office which is busy, we go back to the car and pass a Parish Church which has the sigh, 'born again', we pass two crows standing at a road side, a baby crow with an adult crow. We get into the car and travel back to the bed and breakfast, as we park the car at the bed and breakfast we see a small building beside the house, the building has a lovely door, brick wall and window but no roof, the door leads to no where. We go in and our host looks at our sat sat-nav, he fixes it for us explaining to us about the sound volume which we somehow have manage to switch off. We can now use the sat sat-nav again, afterwards we go to our room.

Life can be like that. Jesus knocks on the door and waits to be let in but we say no. Some of us get into a habit of having a drink which makes us want more, so we have more, a little bit more and so it goes on. The 'dream like' quality of a drink has become a nightmare and we are hooked. When Eve was in the garden God had told her not to eat of the apple. Then Satan, as a serpent said, "Go on Eve it will be all right, you will have more than you will dream of, " Eve was in the Garden of Eden, she ate of the apple, she did not feel better, her dream life had gone and had become a nightmare. Life for her and Adam was never the same again .. and nor for the human race.

Jesus speaks of Himself as the Living Water. The lady at the well spoke to Jesus, "Sir where is this Living Water", and Jesus tells her. The story in John 4:4 onwards tell us that Jesus was sitting by Jacob's well in Samaria while his disciples went to collect some food. Jesus asked her for a drink, the lady was astonished, first she was a Samaritan, Samaritans did not mix with Jews, second she was a woman. He treated her as an equal. Jesus tells her, if you knew the gift of God and who was asking for a drink you would have asked Him and He will give you living water. The lady thinking of the well water was a bit puzzled and wondered how He would take the water out of the well as He did not have a container. She thought about Jacob who built the well and wondered if Jesus was greater than him. Jesus explains that He is the Living Water. The lady asks if she could have this Living Water. She realises that Jesus is different. Jesus tells her she has had five husbands, she realises from what Jesus knows about her, that Jesus is the Messiah. She goes back to her town and tells them what has happened. Many people of the town come to meet Jesus and invited him back stay for two days, many people in that town came to believe that Jesus is the Messiah.

Jesus is always there, turn to Him, He will give you strength to overcome your weaknesses. He is your Living Water, drink of Him and you will never go thirsty.

Madeleine entering the journal from our bedroom overlooking Armagh

The night view is picturesque, the land is like a patch work quilt, the gentle sound of balls go across the pitch. It starts to become dark, the red lights and the lights on the main roads sparkle The cows come gently backwards and forwards across the field. There are baby crows feeding on the grass among the robins, it is indeed a wondrous night.

We travelled 20 miles.

Friday 13 June

We have our breakfast while chatting to a farmer from up North who has come to do an agricultural show in Armagh, which is tomorrow. We hear on the breakfast news that Ireland has voted against the Lisbon Treaty. After breakfast we sit in the lounge looking at the wonderful view, all too soon it is time to leave, we are given a postcard to send home. After saying good-bye to the folk and Shane the dog we set off for Belfast to bring our final proclamation before setting back to England. As we get into the car there are swifts flitting in and out of the half finished room. We listen to the news on the radio, the clearest seems to be Radio 2. Most places here seem to have this station, with the Irish voice of Terry Wogan who blends in well in with all the other Irish voices of the other stations. The sat-nav is speaking beautifully although there seems to be a slight problem as the sat sat-nav suddenly does not tell us which way to turn as we go out, it stays silent.

The sat-nav works only works in registered road yards and begins to talk to us. It is nice not holding the sat-nav close to the ear. Some places in Ireland have kilos, the English like their miles. The Irish too sometimes have different road signs which can be confusing.

As we turn right there is a crucifix on the wall with flowers at Christ's feet. The children are delightful and bring a smile to your face in what they say. As we think of the children, in the Bible, in Mark's Gospel: 13   we are told the disciples rebuked the little children and their parents. Jesus was cross with them and asked them to let the little children come to Him. It is our mission to speak to these little ones and tell them about the God who loves them. So many of these little ones, older children too, are in despair but we can give them hope, hope in Jesus so that they can grow up steady, perhaps one day bring up their own children to the Lord.

We travel on and the sat-nav is chatty. We pass an accident, there is a car in the ditch. Then the phone rings which we answer, it is from the next bed and breakfast. 'Hello it is Lorna here", she chats, "you sound half asleep, are you in still in bed", the sat-nav is competing, we are not sure if she means us or the sat-nav, we arrange times for the next bed and breakfast, we end the conversation that is in a fit of the giggles from all of us. The Irish people have a great sense of humour.

We arrive at the bed and breakfast early, so we wait in their car park. We see a lot of Chaffinches and Magpies, we have some sandwiches and switch on Radio 2, we listen to Jeremy Vine doing interviews about the petrol strike and the news of David Davies resigning from Parliament over Freedom of Speech. There is to be a by-election over this, the other two parties have decided not to contend. While we are listening to the radio there are some bushes in front of us, a little head pokes through, it is a small cub fox. The cub carefully looks around and comes out, the cub is an assortment of orange, brown colours. The cub is so close and very dainty, the cub goes back into the bushes while another one comes out, they pop in and out. While this is happening the cat of the house comes and sits outside watching. Soon it is time to go into the bed and breakfast, we switch off the radio and book into the bed and breakfast, which is a Victorian building. There is a hugh Victorian Bible at the top of the stairs under the table on its ledge. On the wall there a part of a painting which is a picture of God in the cloud with part of His arm reaching out to another hand. In the full picture God is lying on a cloud, modestly covered, reaching his arm out, it is nice to see this. We go to our room and refresh ourselves, we set off and catch a bus to Belfast with our banner. After alighting from the bus, we look round and pray, we find a site in front of a green box and we put up our banner. There is a more relaxed atmosphere with many people shopping. We pray for Christians to come, Our prayers are answered. Colin walks round and is stopped by a Christian on his bicycle, they chat, the cyclist goes to a Methodist Church in Belfast.

While they are speaking a man looks across, he is giving out leaflets, he goes to another corner and comes back. He comes up and says "Hello, God bless you." I explain to him who we are, he goes back to his leafleting, when Colin finishes chatting to the cyclist he goes over to him, they chat and exchange leaflets. The man's name is Jim, he has worked in London for the Open Air Missions and he goes to a Brethren Church in Belfast. He goes into the centre every Friday, he has his photo taken with us. It was so nice to speak to him and the cyclist.

We end our day, take the proclamation down and take a taxi back to the bed and breakfast, the taxi driver is very friendly, we go to bed early as we need take our luggage and get to the ferry early in the morning to take us back to England and Carlisle. It was wonderful to meet Jim doing this work like Paul the Apostle telling people about Jesus. Jesus sent the twelve disciples out to tell others about Him and they did well. The first disciples had Jesus then we have the Holy Sprit who is with us Who leads us to Jesus . We also have the Good News from those early apostles who saw Jesus rise from the dead. We have the Holy Spirit to empower us just as Jesus empowered those young men. "Whom shall I send," asks God. "Here I am Lord send me," Isaiah 6:8. Isaiah did not know Jesus yet he asked God to send him willingly. The disciples had Jesus amongst them for a time, we have the Holy Spirit. When God calls us to do something, we have the faith. "Here I am Lord send me."

Madeleine with street evangelist in Belfast Centre

We travelled 40 miles.

England

Saturday 14 June

We leave Belfast, this is our last day in N Ireland, we are up at 4.00 am to get ready for our journey. We go into the lounge and have a quick breakfast, we have a look at the Message Bible which is on the bookshelves, it is a brilliant translation and introduction to the Bible. It is a good Bible to read to those who have reading problems. We leave at 6 o'clock. We manage to get lost on the ferry road. We are going round loads of lorries and crates wondering where we are going. At last we see another car in front, we manage to speak to them, they are going to the Land ferry and we follow them. At last we get to the ferry terminal and book in. We go to get a drink, on the way in we meet a lady who lives in Belfast and has a sister in Lincoln. We explain that we are from London. It is amazing that people see geographically that Lincoln to us living in London is miles away, while to those living in N Ireland it is the same. We finish our chat and we go upstairs on an escalator as downstairs is where people book. We wait in a queue which seems a long time. There is a group of young people behind us. There are shelves of books for sale on our left. The young people look to decide what books they would like to read on the ship. One young lady said to them, "I like to read my Bible, it is about Jesus," she explained. An announcement is made that we must go to our cars straight away. We leave the queue and cannot find the way out. We find someone who tells us. We go down the stairs out to our cars. As we get back into our car, the car in front of us with an older couple has a Jesus sticker with a fish.

Soon we start to move, we are on the ferry back to England behind the Emerald Green of N Ireland, the beauty of Scotland, Stornoway and its peat, the beautiful mountains with the circling mist, babbling brooks and the sense of humour alongside the Scottish and Irish friendliness. We feel tired, on board we rest. As we sail Ireland slowly goes from view across the sea. A P& O ferry sails slowly across the sea passing us the other way.

We go gently across the sea, soon England is in sight. Again the TV news tells us that the Irish have voted against the Lisbon Treaty. They are celebrating. We drive off the ferry back into England. We are travelling to Carlisle. The countryside is beautiful, we have a wonderful view of country, hills, sea, beautiful beaches. There are clumps of grass on the land. The landscape is changing as we go along. We see sheep and cows. While we are driving we see a sign for 'Faith Mission Centre'.

Faith Mission Centre located between Stranraer ferry and Carlisle

There is a Celtic Cross at the entrance. We stop and go in to see them. We introduce ourselves to Jim Macnealy. We exchange news, Brian and Glen are part of this organisation with their bookshops whom we visited in N Ireland, they run a centre for camping, caravanning, they do tent missions and seminars. While we were here they are doing a Tent Mission. We say "good-bye", take two photos and leave, we drive on greatly encouraged.

Our Journey goes on, we find a restaurant called the Old School House and have our meal outside, there are sheep opposite us on a hill, they are baaing loudly to the sheep on the other side of the road. They eat leaves on trees, we have never seen sheep eat leaves before, in London they normally eat grass. The Old School House was once a small school, there are two buildings here, one houses a cafeteria and clothes, the other building is a photographers called Paul Blackadder, outside this building are the two sinks that the children used. On the original coat hooks are now hung scarves and other clothes for sale. We finish our meal, the mobile phone rings, two people from the Olive Branch are saying "Hello'. After the phone call the bill is paid and we are on our way. We pass Gretna Green. We see on the countryside more windmills. In Stornoway, Scotland there was a protest to stop large ones being built, the people won. Many people do not like the style, one man felt they look like men waving their scrawny arms around.

The sat-nav gets us to our destination and we arrive at the bed and breakfast. We can go in straight away. The bed and breakfast is unusual and has antiques. We refresh ourselves and we walk to Old Scotch Street and Old English Street. We walk through Warwick Street. We take a photo of the castle, go through an archway where we see loads of police cars and there is a constabulary shop. We walk to the square where there is the Salvation Army with a white van profiling their ministry and are in the process of leaving the area. We find a place to put up our banner. A man called Sean comes along, he starts talking. He has belonged to the Full Business Man's Gospel and done evangelism. He claimed in Aberdeen he had a visitation from a down and out man who wanted a lift to England. He gave him a lift. The man used swear words, he believed the man was Jesus. Sean knew a lot about the Bible and Jesus. He liked talking to us because he said that we were gentle. In our opinion this man was deluded and needed help in his relationship with God.

Sean told us a few weeks ago that a preacher preached in a Carlisle Centre. People did not understand him and threw tin cans at him. Sean said the he would rather have someone to speak to him rather that preach at him. Sean leaves. We are finding that young people are interested and that they are intrigued to think that Jesus loves them. There were young men and women who are gothics in their twenties. One with 'I love Monsters' emblazed on her T shirt, they look across the road and are interested. We find again that the ladies are taking leaflets and asking for them. At first we give them out, then we decide to let people ask as the corner is windy and the sun is hot.

Jesus went out to the people, He spoke to them in parables in stories of their every day lives, He spoke to them in their language of Aramaic. He ate, He supped with them, He grew up in the community, He understood where they were coming from, their hopes and their dreams, their trials, their tribulations. One day He had such a great crowd of people who had walked miles to hear Him. They had listened for a long time and were very hungry. Jesus' disciples suggested sending them away into the villages but Jesus said "No". He fed them with five loaves and two fishes with ample food left over. Everyone was satisfied. Matthew 14:13-20.

Jesus today can feed us with His Word. We can be nourished with the Holy Spirit amply again and again. We are perhaps more fortunate than that crowd for we can have Jesus dwelling within us. We do not have to travel for miles or go to a church building to find Him, He is everywhere, we can pray where we want, we can go to our churches to worship together. Do you have a problem, is Jesus your strength in times of trouble? 'Do not put your trust In Princes' the Bible warns, but in God. For mere man can fall. Jesus is your Tower of Strength. Do you know Him, put your trust in Him today, you will never regret it.

We travelled 166 miles that includes 60 miles from Belfast to Stranraer Ferry and then onto Carlisle.

We have a lovely breakfast, the owner has a Scottish lilt, we are reminded that we are on the borders of Scotland and England. There too is a Gideon's Bible in the bedroom, we have a look at the antiques, in the room is an old shop till which the owner had bought from a ship instead of buying a car. Three years ago, in 2005, this road was flooded when the River Eden burst its banks, their house was damaged along with others and all their things were moved upstairs. Across the road an **x** on a house marked shows how high the water rose. We leave the bed and breakfast, we drive through the countryside which is full of sheep. We turn off a main road into a small winding road. We stop at the top where we have a lovely view of the countryside and sheep. We go to have a look at a mother sheep and her lamb but they are not too sure about us and move away from us. They move on and turn to look at us. We get back into the car, we see very cute baby lambs as we go past. Some sheep as elsewhere have coats or have been sheared. We drive on and we notice that there are loads of rabbits along the way, sadly many have been knocked over and make a meal for the crows. The crows too have been knocked down with other types of birds. We find a farm called Brooksbrushes, it is a great place to visit, it is 11 o'clock and busy. They have a restaurant for refreshments and farm shop with a free tractor ride and ice cream. People are sitting on the grass outside and others are buying plants and farm produce. In London we too have farms like this. There is one in Guildford called 'Garstons' which is similar. We leave Brooksbrushes and drive to our bed and breakfast in Newcastle near the centre.

We go into the bed and breakfast, it is very different from Scotland where the front doors are unlocked, here there is CCTV. We are shown the room where we put in our things, we feel something is wrong. We refresh ourselves and go. As we go out and walk down the road a man from the bed and breakfast runs after us, we are in the wrong room, we go back and change rooms. We then leave the hotel and walk to the High Street, along the way it is quiet as it is a Sunday, there are churches around us. We come into the City Centre, it is alive and thronging with people everywhere. We pray for a spot for the banner, we look up and see a plaque on a wall, on the plaque is 'Orphan House Trust, John Wesley erected on this site in 1743. The Orphan House, headquarters of Methodism in the North, City of Newcastle upon Tyne.' This plaque is in between two shops, the Car Phone Warehouse and Priceless shoes . There is history here too in Newcastle County Durham, Richard Neville, known as the King Maker, resided as the Earl of Warwick. He had a great political influence and became the most powerful man in the Country. He had a large estate in Warwickshire through his political manoeuvring. King Henry VI was deposed in 1461 and replaced by King Edward IV who was previously the Duke of York. It was the time of the Wars of the Roses where the houses of the Lancaster and York fought each other, they were represented by roses, the Red Rose for the house of Lancaster, and the White Rose for the House of York. The Earl of Warwick at that time supported the Yorkists. Later Richard Neville changed sides and King Henry VI was put back on the throne. The Earl of Warwick never saw the end of the Wars of the Roses, which ended in 1485, when Richard III and Henry Tudor a Welsh man and the Earl of Richmond who with the Welsh people marched into England and fought Richard III in the Battle of Bosworth Field in Leicestershire. King Richard III died and his crown was taken from a thorn bush and placed upon Henry Tudor's head making him King Henry VII. Richard Neville Earl of Warwick was killed in a battle in 1471 fighting against the man whom he had put on the throne Edward IV.

Plaque above shop in Newcastle Centre

We find a spot outside a Primarks store against a wall next to their windows opposite Marks and Spencers. We set up the banner, a man comes up and points out the commandment 'Thou shalt not lie'. He seems to have a problem with this commandment, then he leaves.

We stand and wait. Peruvian music drifts across the square, they wear red blanket style clothes which brings a brilliant colour to their music, it sounds like the wind across the trees. People watch the musicians. After the IRA bombings in the 1980's we went shopping in Hounslow, west London, and the Peruvians were playing their music. They played 'Amazing Grace', the town went silent, no-one moved, it was as if time stood still. A young woman, beside me, in her twenties sang the words quietly, Amazing Grace rang across that square. The music ended and everything went back to normal.

As the music continues to drift across the square where we are standing we have the sense of being invisible, of Jesus being on the Cross with people passing Him by. As in the days of Noah they will be shopping, drinking, given in marriage. One day Jesus will close the door and they will never enter. We see a young man with a T shirt with the words 'soul on fire.' Another man passes by with a skull & crossbones printed on his T shirt. At this point Jesus spoke to me within saying, "They do not see Me, they pass Me by." We think of Moses the Lawgiver, then two Jewish men pass by. People look and again women take leaflets and young people look, there is a mixture of people of decent, African, Saudi Arabian, Indian, Pakistan, Chinese walking up and down the street. There is representation from many nations. A young lady comes and takes a photo of us on her mobile. We take turns to hold the banner. We see smartly dress African, Caribbean people passing by, we can see that they are Christians. A man passes by with his guitar. We greet one family on their way to church. We finish our afternoon and put away our banner. We go home by taxi.

The taxi driver tells us about a protest by an organisation called 'Fathers for Justice' which is for men who are separated from their children and are fighting to have rights to see their children. Apparently the men climbed over the bridge which is over the river and put a dummy with a noose round its neck, the police thought it was a real person and so did the drivers going over so all traffic was affected. Earlier in the week this organisation had spent three days on MP Harriet Harman's roof. The driver is, as many others we have met, very friendly, he talks about football. He drops us off outside the bed and breakfast.

Today's outreach was interesting, we are reminded of the Vine, "I Am the Vine, you are the branches and God is the Gardener." We see in Genesis 9 :20 that Noah, when he came off the Ark, was was given a vineyard. He became a gardener pruning away dead branches that did not produce good fruit. In John 15:5 we are again reminded of this. God is the gardener He cuts off any dead branches and prunes others so that they will become more fruitful. The branches are us. If we remain in Jesus and He in us we can do great things. For those who do not produce fruit God cannot use and they are cast off. God is the pruner and He longingly looks after us. We only have to do as He asks us to do and have faith to do what He wants. He sent His Son to die for our sins, Jesus died and rose again. Jesus sent the Comforter, the Holy Spirit. How wonderful it is to know that we have a friend, a friend who never leaves us. "I will never leave you nor forsake you." That is His promise today and forever. Amen.

We travelled 50 miles from Carlisle to Newcastle.

We have a breakfast at the bed and breakfast, there are four of us in the breakfast room.

We leave the room and put our luggage into the car. We meet a man from Brentford who is staying in the bed and breakfast, Brentford is in the London Borough of Hounslow. He is on his way back to Brentford. He had come for the cricket, we speak about the Rugby ground in Twickenham and the concerts that are played there. The Bees who are footballers for Brentford are waiting for a new ground to play football on, he is a fervent follower of Brentford. We put our luggage into the car, we say "good-bye" to him, we are on our way.

We make our way, the sat nav is not sure where it is going. We pass over the bridge where the prank with the 'Fathers for Justice' dummy had taken place, there is a police presence. We see two radio stations advertised Magic FM and Century FM. As we start to travel a building has on the walls 'Have Faith in God'. We travel along and we see two shops.

We also see the Angel of the North, he is huge, he can be seen for miles, he is an impressive figure.

This is a contemporary sculpture designed by Antony Gormley, which is located in Gateshead, England. As the name suggests, it is a steel sculpture of an angel, standing 66 feet (20 m) tall, with wings measuring 178 feet (54 m) across making it wider than the Statue of Liberty's height. The wings themselves are not planar, but are angled 3.5 degrees forward, which Gormley has said aims to create "a sense of embrace". It stands on a hill, on the southern edge of Low Fell overlooking the A1 road and the A167 road into Tyneside and the East Coast Main Line rail route.

We get to Richmond York, we drive through this pretty town, park the car and take it in turns to look for a place to put the banner. Richmond York is a

Barrack town, there is a museum about the Army. We decide to go to the bed and breakfast where we are greeted by Judith our hostess who has lived in west London and she knows Ealing. She tells us a story about her husband going shopping for eggs and being served with William Haigh as this is his constituency here.

Finkle Street in Richmond Yorkshire

We go into our room and change. We set off for Finkle Street and put up the banner opposite 'Help The Aged' charity shop. We wait, a lady comes up on her bicycle, she has been for thirty years a school RE and PE teacher, she has travelled extensibly across the world and the Middle East and is able to speak Hebrew and Arabic. She went to school in Richmond. She confessed to a faith but not a solid one but seen from our point of view erroneous. She has a strong quest for spiritual things, she has been baptised a Methodist, she goes to a Church of England in Richmond.

Richmond Centre

One of her friends passed and said "God bless you" to encourage us. They leave, a white van pulls up opposite an upstairs shop windows open. The shop presses clothes, huge tubes come from the windows onto the van, rubbish is passed down through the tubes onto the white van. The tubes are put away and the van goes. We finish the outreach, pick up our banner, we look round the town. The Market Place is very pretty, there are plenty of taxis here for people, there are general shops such as Woolworths and Somerfields and is well served for people who like clothes. There are many soldiers here, they belong to the Kings Own Scottish Regiment, they come and go with their families. it is a friendly town, there is too, Richmond Castle.

King's Own Scottish Border Regiment

The King's Own Scottish Border Regiment was mustered in 1689, originally called the Earl of Leven's. The Borderers' military history dates back to honours in Namur in 1695, Gallipoli in 1915-16 and Dunkirk in 1940. During the turbulent days of 1689, when the citizens of Edinburgh were in a state of alarm at the prospect of an attack by Jacobite forces, David Earl of Leven was authorised 'with all expedition to levie one Regiment of Foot'. This he achieved in the remarkably short period of two hours. Named after him initially as 'Leven's Regiment', it was soon to be in action at the Battle of Killiecrankie. But this was not to be the Regiment's last conflict with the Jacobites, for it is unique in the Army in having also fought at Sherriffmuir in 1715 and at Culloden in 1746. The King's Own Scottish Borderers are one of the six infantry regiments which 'gained immortal glory' at the Battle of Minden in 1759 by advancing against a superior force of French Cavalry. This battle commemorated annually on the first of August when the Regiment wear red roses in their head-dress following the tradition that the soldiers had picked roses as they advanced through gardens before the battle. This custom was even observed by Borderers in 1944 when they mounted an attack on Minden Day during the invasion of Normandy - for they attached to their helmets the roses which they plucked from the hedgerows. During the last fifty years the King's Own Scottish Borderers have seen action in Palestine, Korea, Malaya, Aden, Borneo and The Gulf.

About a mile from Richmond Yorkshire John Wycliffe, the English Reformer, was born in 1330 at a place called Hipswell. He was a Roman Catholic and he started to speak against the Catholic Church and firmly believed that people should be able to read the Bible themselves instead of the priests reading it to them. He believed that Christians should read the Bible in their own language. He translated the Vulgate Bible into English. He was a teacher at Oxford University and started a movement called Lollardy, the members' were encouraged to translate the Bible into English. He and the Lollards had a tough time and many gave up as the government and church persecuted them. John Wycliffe himself had a stroke and died in 1384 but some people continued to carry on what he believed in even though some people were burnt to death. In the 1600's the Reformation came and alongside it the Protestant movement. Protestant beliefs were very smilier to what John Wycliffe believed, he is sometimes regarded as the founder of Protestantism in England.

The Bible has many translations that people can use today to understand what God is saying into today's world. Many translators are working in other languages so that others may read the Bible in their own native tongue. The Message Bible translation is an example of introducing others to the Bible in simple language so that they will be able to read the Bible and understand it.

In the book of Genesis we are reminded why there are different languages, Genesis 11:13. The whole world had one language and common speech but man wanted to build a massive tower and a city up to the Heavens and make himself great and a reluctance to spread across the world as God desired. God realised that if men did this they would have pride and have no need of Him. So He went and gave them different languages so they could not communicate with each other, thus they were scattered. In the book of Acts 2 when the Holy Spirit came down the disciples spoke in tongues. Jewish people from all the nations had come to Jerusalem. They had spread out across the world and did not all speak the same language. Jesus Himself spoke about three languages. They were amazed that Peter was speaking in all the languages to them, along with the other Apostles, and they understood. God had used Pentecost for people to understand His Word in their languages. In Genesis man was was scattered, his tongue changed. In the Book of Acts Peter and the others spoke in all the languages about God and Jesus their Saviour. Is it not marvellous that in Christ we become as one whilst in the secular world we are divided and lost with Satan as our head. We thank God that Jesus has used translators and the printing press so that all can read and understand the scriptures. In the UK and all over the world.

We travelled 47 miles from Newcastle to Richmond Yorkshire.

Tuesday 17 June

Today we say cheerio to Judith who has looked after us so well. Her husband works in the Army as a Recruitment Officer. We hear on the radio that where we were standing in Fingle Street that there is to be a parade down Fingle Street into the Market Place to welcome the soldiers back from Afghanistan to give them the Freedom of the City on Friday afternoon.

We drive away from Richmond with its quaint surroundings, as we drive away we see a woman put on washing on a line across the pavement. We have only seen this in pictures, mainly of London years ago. As we drive along we see three flags, two of St George and a Scottish flag in the middle. We stop at another farm which has an assortment of animals, an apricot camel, lamas, accapalas, bulls, sheep, cows who are very docile and quiet until a lady comes out with their meal. There is a farm shop which sells beautiful hand made jewellery, hats, chocolate etc., it is a new shop, it has been not been open long. There is a cafeteria nearby run by the farm, a queue of people who have arrived by coach are here already waiting to get in. It is a good place to visit. Soon we leave the farm and pass on the way another farm called Thorpe Farm Cafe with a picnic area and then Westmoreland Farm Cafe and also Orton Village. There are plenty of bed and breakfasts here and refreshment areas depending on what you require. We pass Egglestone Abbey.

We drive to Eden, a place in Yorkshire and go to have a meal in the The Mulberry Bush which is a cafeteria. It is packed with tourists and looks a nice place to eat. In fact we have to wait outside. The locals were eating takeaways outside and one lady speaks to us, "Don't you feel sorry for us having to eat outside, we are waiting for the bus which is collecting us at 11.30 am." The people here are very friendly and humorous. While we are waiting we have a look around the town. A church building which looked as though it has been a Church of England building has become a shopping centre. You walk through the doors where the priest would have greeted the parishioners and to your left is alcohol. On the right hand side are every day goods and a rope across the stairs to the balcony. Further on as you walk towards the front there are honeys and jams. Right in front of you where the altar has been is the local Post Office, as you go to the Post Office and turn right there are cards for sale with goods to your left. The floor has stayed the same and you can imagine the people worshipping here, it feels very strange. We go back to the Mulberry Bush for our meal which is slowly filling with cyclists and others. There is Beatle music being played.

Travelling between Richmond Yorkshire to Kendal Cumbria

Then we continue on our Journey. We notice the difference in landscape, it is much greener here. There are lakes with grass plains although not Irish Green. We find the bed and breakfast and unload, we refresh ourselves and go to Kendal Market place. Gill, the manager, has very kindly invited us to stand outside her Christian Bookshop in the town centre. Gill takes us in for refreshments and prayer inside the shop. Her assistant is serving while we pray for each other. Gill has been an art teacher and she has only been in the shop for six months. Gill's assistant is from an evangelical background and is at the moment attending a Methodist Church. During prayer we have a vision of a crystal within the bookshop, it is alight with many colours. After prayer we go outside on a hill and it is blowy.

Tuesday is not a market day so there will probably be fewer people, there is a pub opposite us call the George and Dragon. The people here are friendly and warm. We meet a few Christians and a nice Catholic man who is full of the faith. We meet a lady from St Thomas Church of England in Kendal.

A Christian lady who lives thirty miles from Gloucester stops and gives us a poem she has written. She prays for us and goes. A man is putting up posters, he is in his mid twenties. We chatted to him about faith, He has looked at different faiths. He had studied physics, as far as Christianity is concerned, finds it full of contradictions. He is a friendly man. He has been confirmed and brought up in church, he leaves and we speak to a few Christians in and out of the shop. We catch the eye of a few thousand passers by although not a busy day. A man comes by with a lady in a wheelchair. We ask if they would like a leaflet. The lady says "yes," he says "no," The lady takes the leaflet, "you took it, you can read it" he says angrily.

We have enjoyed our day, we say good-bye to Gill and we have a photo taken, we go back to the bed and breakfast. Thinking about the man pushing the wheelchair. We can from this remember the Pharisees and Sadducees who were always telling Jesus off, they did not like the tax collectors who were despised, or the prostitutes or anyone who they felt beneath them, they were very keen to keep themselves pure and clean. If their robes were touched they would have a thorough wash as they felt tainted. Both John the Baptist and Jesus told them that they had to be clean on the inside as well as the outside in their thoughts, words and deeds. One day they said to Jesus disciples, "Why does your teacher eat with these people?" Jesus replied, "It is not the healthy who require a doctor, it is the sick." Matthew 9:11. The Pharisees and Sadducees did not see themselves as sinners but beyond reproach. People like the prostitutes and tax collectors knew that they had sinned and repented. Jesus warned that the prostitutes and tax collectors would come first in the Kingdom of God before the Pharisees and Sadducees.

Is it not wonderful that no matter what we have done we can turn to God and say sorry, we are forgiven. What a wonderful God. Amen.

Christian Bookshop in Kendal, Cumbria

Kendal High Street

We travelled 61 miles from Richmond Yorks to Kendal in Cumbria.

Wednesday 18 June

   Last night there was a storm and the rain was heavy, a house alarm went off, we did not sleep very well. One area had four inches of rain according to the radio. Our hostess did not notice anything, she had slept through it. At breakfast we met her husband, he is jolly. After breakfast we get ready to leave. The houses here are made of stone and are solid, as we are on the top floor there is a wonderful view of rooftops and countryside with trees and sheep in the distance. When it starts to go dark you are reminded of Mary Poppins, you expect Julie Andrews and Dick Van Dyke to appear and sing on the rooftops. The windows look as if they have come out of Dickens London, you can imagine snow settling on them.
   As we are packing we look out of the window. There is a wonderful view of a flock of birds that form shapes in the sky, they are swifts, other birds join in as they fly making shapes of balls and oblongs. They fly here and there in absolute formation. They are dark but as they flew down the sunlight catches them as they fly down to the fields. We can only describe it like white lights glistening on the blue sea. Sometimes it seems that they are invisible then as they came up the whites on their plumage shine. It was breathtaking. Soon we are on our way.

View from our bedroom before leaving our B&B

We pass the English countryside and Sizargh castle, there is another farm/teashop and crafts, there seems to be plenty of places to stop and eat. We stop at a coffee shop for refreshments and go on our way. We see another English flag on the way. We also pass a cafe called Hideaway Coffee House. We are having problems with the sat-nav so we are working out our own way. We notice that it is trying to rain. We also noticed as in Stornoway that some stone houses are being left to fall into disuse. Although we notice in one area that some stone houses are being completely renovated with new roofs and other refurbishment's, with so many people badly in need of homes perhaps that is better. We pass a pig sty , we see a mum with her piglets, she has her own shelter, we notice that mum and her piglets are like a dark velvet. We notice too that some of the sheep are a very dark chocolate almost black. Some have spotted black heads. We arrive into York which is called the Walled City.

We find our bed and breakfast where we are welcome by Wendy. Soon we are on our way to York City Centre. York has many tourists and school children, people are travelling everywhere, it is part pedestrianised. We pray and search for a place to put our banner. While we are looking we see a BBC van for Radio York and a van for Sky TV, there is a street market. The old and new parts of the street blend into one. We see young men in a blue grey tartan. People call each other 'Pet'. There is such a blend of accents here as tourists, visitors and others join in. We set our banner behind the church on the pavement, people pass and look but there is little response. We see a lady go by dressed in 1930's style with a turban. Young women with boyfriends do tend to look. Our observation was that they seem to realise that a love can go beyond a love of a male, that there is something more. It starts to rain, the wind is blowing and we pray for it to stop and soon it does. A young man passes us, he turns round points at us and shouts "Get on your knees and pray." Eventually we put our banner away and go home.

When Jesus sent the twelve disciples out to evangelise he told them to take no cloak, money, bag, or bread. We too as Christians must evangelise, we need to let everyone know of the Good News of the Bible, it is up to the person if they accept or reject the Good News of the Gospel. If we have spent time with that person and they are not going to change we must then go and tell others as well. We can pray for that person but if all our time is spent on them and not one else has heard the Good News of Jesus then a lot of people will be left who could have been saved. Jesus told His disciples to move on if they were ignored. Go to as many people as you can, do not waste time on those who have heard the word and do not want it, go to others who are ready to receive the Word. Jesus Himself went to His home town of Nazareth and visited the local synagogue, He read the scripture of Isaiah 61 telling the people that He was the Messiah, they were so angry they drove Him out of the synagogue through the town to a cliff and tried to throw him over the edge. Luke 4:14-28. Sometimes your family will not receive you or your friends but pray for them all and others that they may know the truth and they shall be free indeed.

We travelled 86 miles from Kendal in Cumbria to York in North Yorkshire.

Thursday 19 June

We say good-bye to Wendy. Here the houses have changed, they are made of brick. We leave the bed and breakfast fairly early and set off for Liverpool, wondering what it will be like. The countryside is pretty and also the green reflecting onto the lakes. We drive along and the sun peers through a cloud and lights the land, it is beautiful. We pass a place called Lutheran Hall and aware that we are passing through Bronte country we are reminded of Charlotte, Anne, Emily and their brother Patrick Bramwell living with their father, Rev Patrick Bronte, who was a parson of the local church in Haworth. From this place we have people talk of the Yorkshire Moors as desolate but today they are ablaze with colour. From this place we have the wonderful legacy of the stories that these sisters wrote. Jane Eyre and Wurthering Heights perhaps the best known. It is incredible to think that in those days women were not supposed to write and the three sisters had to send male relatives and friends in to pretend that they were the writers. Today we have so many stories written by female writers. We cross the Pennine Chain. The land as we go along looks like a portrait painting as if the trees have been painted onto the hills by a giant hand. There is also Aintree race course. Soon we come into Liverpool, the sat-nav guides us in. As you drive in you are reminded of London, like a lot of cities it is being regenerated. Loads of houses are being boarded up, we pass a junior school, according to the adverts on the buses the education in Liverpool is very good and one can imagine so. It is a City of change. We come to the bed and breakfast, this one has a CCTV, the front door is locked, there is a reception desk. In the bedroom there is a security safe. We refresh ourselves and go into the railway station. We go onto the train which is very comfortable, you are welcomed on board by the computer. The computer lets you know where you are going and where to get off. There are notices telling you not to put your feet on the seats. We ask a gentleman where to get off for our stop. He tells us, we alight from the train and head for Liverpool centre.

Liverpool is buzzing with people, we look round and pray for a spot. We go and have refreshments at the local British Home Store cafeteria. We eat outside, the weather is very hot. There are ladies passing in beautiful coloured Pakistani dress, there are many types of people here and many ladies are wearing thirties style dresses. We see tartan skirts. We see signs on bins as in the other cities indicating you will be fined, in this case £75, and for your cigarettes there are trays on the bins to stub out cigarettes. There are always signs just outside the cities to tell you that CCTV is watching you. We have a nice lunch, we go to see where the Beatles played in the Cavern. We are told the Cavern Walk is now a shopping centre.

Liverpool Centre

We find a spot for our banner, this time opposite Primark, it is very sunny as we set up the banner. On our left is a flautist playing with his dog beside him. A man comes along and looks at the map on the banner, he chats about him mum and tells us she was born in Scotland, his dad was in the forces, they met and went to live in Liverpool where he was born. On our map of the United Kingdom, right at the top is a place called Hogwarts, he is going to look it up as he has never heard of it as he is interested in Scottish places. He has relatives in Scotland whom he goes to see. He says good-bye and goes.

Another gentleman comes, he is in his sixties, he is a widower, and has lost his wife two years ago. He is not interested in money, he feels that the world is too materialistic. He does not have a lot himself, he has no home or material possessions and misses his wife, he cannot understand why people want so much. He realises that money cannot bring happiness and would give it to help others. He asks if we are religious but we say "no", that we have a personal faith. Christianity is by faith and not by works and a Christian has a personal relation with God through Jesus Christ who is God. God is triune, Father, Son and Holy Spirit, three persons being one God. While this man is speaking another man comes up. We pray that the man we are speaking to would have the Word of God. The prayer is answered, the man coming up is a Christian and tells him about receiving Jesus into his life as a personal Saviour. The widower said that he was not a bad man but had done wrong in his life. While this was happening two men come along, they are from Sri Lanka and homeless. One has travelled from Scotland and the other from London. The one from London was with his girlfriend, he is selling the Big Issue. He asks about the Trinity which was explained out to him and he understands. He seems to know his Bible. He says he has asked Christians on the street this question before, they did not seem to know their Bible or about the Trinity. He goes, leaving his friend with us. His friend asks what is on the banner as he cannot not read English, he shows us his crucifix round his neck. We gather that his mother was a Pentecostal Catholic, but he does not like Pentecostal worship. While this is going on the other two men who were speaking have finished their conversation. The non Christian leaves, the Christian man starts to chat. His name is Ken, he is just fifty years old. He has lived in Liverpool a long time. He normally preaches in Liverpool High Street but he is unwell at the moment. He was 'born again' through his mother having a Bible in the house. His dad was not a believer. At the age of nineteen he read the Book of Revelation and became a believer. He then says, "good-bye, God bless you."

We chat a little more to the homeless man, he then leaves. The first homeless man comes back. He lives with his girlfriend in a friends house. He claims to be a Christian. He knows he makes wrong decisions. He has been selling the Big Issue for two years, he cannot work at the moment as for people like himself it takes seven years, this is a government ruling he says. We feel that he has the beginning of a relationship with the Lord. A lady comes up in her eighties and tells us, "The Lord you can trust."

At five o'clock a group of four young men come along with trumpet, drum and guitar. They start playing and they sing Beatles songs. A blond woman comes with them, she chats on her mobile phone and leaves. People move fast towards them, purses open and money is flung onto the hat on the ground. They are smiling, happy. Would it not be lovely if people got as excited about God and praised His name and realised who gave those young men their gift of music. We fold up the banner and leave, we are stopped by a man in a cult, we chat and go, we pass shops with pictures of the Beatles, we see John Lennon Street. We see a funny looking bunch of models of the Beatles with heads bobbing up and down in the window as as we go by. There is also a Christian Bookshop. We board the train back to the bed and breakfast. We are impressed by the friendliness of the City and the concern of people for one another, the two homeless men spoke of the friendliness and help that they had received in Liverpool. This leads us onto another command of Jesus, "Love one another as I have loved you." Do not love others that love you but include everyone. On the Cross Jesus said, "Father forgive them." Jesus also tells us to love our neighbour as ourselves. It is not easy to love one another when people are rude. We are always reminded of Mother Theresa who had a great love for her fellow men. She would take the homeless and also monks off the streets in India, carry them into a sanctuary wash them clean with such love. These monks had been men who had mocked her for being a Christian. They would worship in their temples. When they were not much use anymore they would be left lying on the streets. They could not understand why she helped them. She would tell them about Jesus the one who died for them. How her hands and feet were Christ's. It is hard to love some people, the prostitutes, the drunkards, but we can with Christ's help, we can through love tell them about Jesus, how much He loves them. To have the boldness to go into our streets, bars, night-clubs and tell people that Jesus loves them. It is a hurting World out there but like Isaiah says, "Whom shall I send?" asks the Lord. "Here I am Lord, Send me," Isaiah responds.

We travelled 99 miles from York to Liverpool.

Friday 20 June

Travelling between Liverpool to Sheffield

Today we say farewell to Liverpool and we are on our way to Sheffield. We travel along the motorway. The weirs are stunning as we pass on the motorway. You can also see the windmills on the horizon with industrial funnels. it is an industrial city with foundries of the past and windmills of the present. We arrive at the next bed and breakfast which has a view of the countryside. The views in Scotland, Ireland and England are varied, beautiful and unique in their own ways. We see sheep as we pass. Scotland, her mountains and heather. Ireland for its deep rich greens, England's hillsides with different shades of greens varying from the others, here the trees are a dark green, the green fields growing light and dark as the sunlight passes over. In the distance to our right are houses and to our left funnels showing again the progress of time from agriculture to industry. The cluster of houses have been built for industry. Indeed the bed and breakfast reminds us of the Trade Union Movement for workers in the shops, mines and the hard work of those days. The early Socialists who went on their bikes to get votes and became what is the Labour Party today. Here too is where the Sheffield Steel industry came into being. While we wait to book in we have a walk round the gardens which are lovely and peaceful. There is a Lavender Garden with a dry fountain with a figure of a woman with two dolphins. Soon we return to reception to book in for our room. We refresh ourselves and have a meal there. We are seated in a lounge near a wedding party where people are eating before going to the ceremony. The lounge is full of people going to meetings and seminars. Others are seated outside enjoying the sunshine.

Trade Union Movement Conference Centre in Sheffield

Soon it is time to leave and we drive off to Sheffield centre. We find a car park and go to the city by foot. We walk into town, we go up a long hill. There is a new building site which is a bit derelict. There are shops here that are closed. One is a kitchen shop which has loads of broken grass, there is a spot with a narrow pathway and long grass. There is a tram line in the middle of the main road and loads of rubble as the trams go up and down.

Sheffield Shopping Centre

We turn into a square, there are loads of flats for students down the road leading from the square. We meet a student who very kindly walks with us to the town and shows us where to go. He is married, he and his wife have visited the London Eye, he is studying physics. He then leaves and we enter the City and pray for a spot for the banner. We find a spot and put up the banner. This afternoon is interesting as our banner is near a group of Christians preaching on our left. A lady too is playing her guitar to our right. We manage to go over and talk to the Christians. We introduce ourselves. One of the team members is a man called Jim Gourlary who came from the Living Waters Fellowship, they go nearly every Friday to the City Centre where they are preaching. It is a hub bub of people, people of all ages and faiths are chatting to each other or at the preacher asking questions, it is like a market place, people working in shops came out to have a look, it is amazing. Some people get heated but they let off steam and are ok. A lady letting off steam commented, "What with you and them lot up there," she commented pointing our way.

As we stood with the banner a lady comes across, gives us the sign of the Cross and says "God bless you," and goes. A man called Paul comes along and chats, he is from the Methodist Church, he tells us he is doing the Ten Commandments with his home group. A lady called Jean with a male friend comes along from the New Testament Church of God, she speaks to us. Jean speaks of the banner encouraging her and the Word, this seems to be speaking to her. Jean also tells us that some Christians and a Christian lady pray for people at bus stops. They say good-bye and leave. A Chinese lady comes along with a pusher filled with toys, balloons, scarves. She takes out a foot pump and blows up the balloons, a balloon bursts and makes everyone jump. The balloons have a rattle sound as they are shaken, as children pass they listen. The Chinese lady is looking hard at the banner. A group of people come past in bin liners, emphasising the point of recycling your bags. After this The British Heart Foundation comes along with heart shaped red buckets to collect money. Another lady comes past and gives the thumbs up sign. We meet a very excited Christian who is in his fifties. He jokes about the other Christian group having a bigger audience. Colin explains that we all have different gifts but God uses us all in our different ways. In the meantime a young lad tries to take three balloons off the Chinese ladies pusher, the lady grips his wrist quite hard until he lets go. Another lady comes down the street singing the hymn, 'How Great Thou Art.' After this a man called Peter comes up and introduces himself, he is a student, he has just married, he is in the Jesus Army. He has been with them but like us his gifting is not preaching but he likes evangelising. Peter leaves and we put away our banner.

Sheffield Centre

We take a taxi back to the car park in Ebernezar Square, the driver cannot find it so we have a tour of Sheffield. We are advised to ask a traffic co-ordinator who writes it down for us. We find a taxi driver who knows where it is. We gratefully get back into our car. We drive the nine miles back, we pass a building which has been painted with a blue background with parrots, it is very good. We buy some sandwiches on the way. We stop before going into the bed and breakfast. Where we are sitting near us is a church, a few houses, there is also a small post office and a tuck shop, while we are eating there is a lady rider and horse. It is very pretty here. We finish our sandwiches and drive to the bed and breakfast. As we enter the bed and breakfast we see in the local newspaper complaints about the new windmills.

When we think about Christians today, we think about evangelism. We think of Jesus. Jean was touched in a way she had not been touched before by the words on the banner. We are reminded that the Word, the Bible is Holy. John's Gospel is the most profound, 'In the beginning was the Word, and the Word was with God, and the Word was God. He was with God in the beginning.' When God created the World in Genesis, it says, through His Word the World was created. The first thing that God speaks of is, "Let there be light." John says, 'In Him was life, that life was the Light of men. He separates the light from the darkness. The light shines in the darkness but the darkness has not understood it.'

Isaiah 17:7 onwards was given to us, 'In that day men will look to their Maker and turn their eyes to the Holy One of Israel. They will not look to the altars, the work of their hands, and they will have no regard for the Asherah poles, and the incense altars their fingers have made.' We can see the second of the Ten Commandments is 'You shall not make for yourself an idol.' There are dire warnings about this in the Bible and in Isaiah 17:10, 'You have forgotten the Lord your Maker. '

Our World, our Nation is lost, it has turned away from God. We as Christians have the answer, that answer is Jesus. It is not the denomination we belong to, the church cannot save us. It is the Word, the Light of the World, who came and died upon the Cross for us. Wherever we are it is the faith in Jesus that unites us as brothers and sisters in Christ, not the church, however good our church is, it cannot save us. Only Jesus can do that. 'Put not your trust in princes but in God.' Mere man cannot save you.

We travelled 84 miles from Liverpool to Sheffield in South Yorkshire.

Saturday 21 June

Today we leave Sheffield for Nottingham. We have breakfast looking at the country view. We load up the car and see a crow feeding a young crow. We drive away enjoying the view of the countryside. There is a field covered in red poppies. The weather has been wet but it does not take away the beauty of the countryside. There are still sheep in the fields lying down. It is interesting to note as we travel that we see the Narnia film Prince Caspian on posters, in various towns, showing at their cinemas. We see this poster in Nottingham. This is Robin Hood country and there is Nottingham Castle for people to see. There are many trees which you notice when you have travelled down from Scotland and Ireland. Scotland is a land of mountains and clear water so pure to drink it looks like crystal, it is beautifully soft. As you come down to England there are more and more trees of varying greens. The flag of St George is always flying as you travel on. The Scottish accent has dwindled although you can still hear hear the Scottish accent occasionally and see the occasional kilt. We have also seen in England men wearing trues or kilts of red tartan. The Scottish weddings are very colourful, the bride wears a tartan sash across her wedding dress. We arrive at the bed and breakfast. We book in and walk to Nottingham. We pass three churches and a church school. This is an amazing centre. Like the other cities it has its own uniqueness. There are thousands and thousands of people here, like Sheffield there are trams.

We walk into the square. There is a farmers market, there are vans and stalls and they are covered over by canopies. There is a water fountain with water gushing out. We walk round and pray for a site. We hear loud singing, a group of young women are singing and dancing on the wall while others are giving out leaflets. Later on a male joins them. We go over and introduce ourselves. These young Christians go almost every Saturday proclaiming the Good News of Jesus, it is wonderful to see. After chatting to the Christians we go for a meal in the local Marks & Spencer. As we go in we see a man singing with a guitar, he sings Elvis Presley songs and sounds like him. We have lunch and go back to the square. We put up our banner. The place is teeming with young people. We have never seen so many young people in one place. The Community Police keep an eye on them. The styles they wear are varied. There is Gothic style, Sixties style. Victorian style. Jeans, all manner of dress. Two ladies come up and ask us where Marks & Spencer is. Then a Christian comes up with his Bible, he is wearing a badge 'Jesus Saves.' He does not seem sure of his faith and asked us to show him Jesus. We explained that Jesus is within us. He was not too sure about this and said pointing at the banner "Hmm, you should have put all the laws down," and walked off. We prayed for him. Another man went past and said to his female companion, "Jesus loves you.'

People look at the banner as they go past. There is a newsagents opposite. A market stall is selling loads of scarves with brightly coloured umbrellas covering the scarves. A man is playing music down the way. Young people keep gazing at the banner while they are chatting. A group of men pose in costumes for charity. A group of women too go by in costume across the street. A man goes past dressed as a donkey with three other men carrying cameras. He comes back again and poses for photos with the young people. Two young men are jousting each other on other young men's backs and keep falling off. The rain comes down, the umbrella is put up, it is interesting to watch the activity here. We decide to take the banner down and go. We see a group of men being photographed at the fountain as we go past, one actually goes in and swims, people are chasing each other laughing in the water. A man takes a photo.

Nottingham Centre

Two young women decide to do the same and take a swim in the fountain. When we think about the fountains we are reminded that we can paddle in our faith with Jesus or we can be fully immersed in Jesus and receive all that He desires for our lives. Jesus is the Fountain of Life. It is up to us to make that choice, as Jesus said to Nicodemus, "You must be born again."

We take a taxi to the bed and breakfast. When we arrive at the bed and breakfast we look at the internet for The Eye FM, it is very good, we are having an interview there tomorrow on route to Peterborough.

We travelled 44 miles from Sheffield to Nottingham.

Sunday 22 June

Today we listen to the BBC Radio, it is very interesting, it is about Gypsy folk in France, they now have fifty two Christian churches in France. They are finding faith in Jesus and are being baptised. Many were not wanted in the local churches. They are now recognised by the French Government. We hear too about the Black Churches in England and how they came into being. They had the same problem as the Gypsies in France. The Church of England could not cope with black people so the Black Churches came in. Rev Rose Hudson speaks, she has been a Christian for ten years, ten people walked out of her services in Church because she was a woman and black, despite this her

Church has grown. There is also talk of the Anglican Church in Jerusalem, of the meeting of Bishops who do not wish to meet in England at the synod with the other bishops over the issue of sexuality.

We go down to breakfast and drive off to The Eye FM for an 11-12.00 pm interview. This is a community station, it reaches thousands of people in the Nottingham and Leicester area. It has fifteen presenters who are all volunteers. Christine and Patrick are chief executors. Jerry is a presenter who is interviewing us with Patrick today. The radio station is run from a house. We stop by a field and we ring Christine by our mobile who very kindly gives us directions. We try to listen to the station in the car but as usual it is very difficult to get stations. Sometimes you can get a local station but it is not always easy. We are now able to get Radios 4, 2, 3 and Five Live, other stations are not so easy to tune into. We pass cows that are white coloured. There is a smell of burning, the smell is coming from council offices that have recently been burnt down.

The Eye FM Radio Station with Madeleine and Patrick

We arrive at The Eye FM radio station, it is about halfway to Peterborough. We see a big mast by the house, their other mast is on a farm about one mile away. We are warmly welcomed by Christine, we meet Patrick and the station cat who is snoozing on a chair near us. Christine tell us that the population listening is up to a million people. She also tells us that the council offices burning down were big news about three weeks ago. Christine leaves us. We sit down outside the studio and listen to Patrick, Jerry and guest, the interview is first class. We meet the interviewee on his way out. Christine takes us in and we are introduced to Jerry. One of the chairs is very high for me but I manage to sit on it. Jerry tries to get it to go lower but the chair just stays the same height. We open a door in the studio as it is very hot. We get ready for the interview. Christine pops in and chats. The interview starts, Christine goes and we are away, we enjoy ourselves, all too soon it is over. We take photos of each other, then we are on our way. If you live in Nottingham, Leicester do listen in it is a good radio station. Christine has arranged on Sunday mornings a pause for thought for five minutes, presented by the leaders of churches, so you never know, your own church leader may be on. Pray for this ministry that it will reach people listening. Christine was saying that the minister that morning was talking about pruning his hedge and he needed a ladder. He used the ladder. He then spoke about Jesus being our ladder. Christine was impressed by this. Radio is a great vehicle for telling people about Jesus. If you are invited to chat on Radio stations do take this opportunity for many people will be blessed by what you say. Someone may even become a Christian through your witness.

Rutlands Lakes in the Barns Dale travelling to Peterborough

We have a lovely drive through Barns Dale and the Rutlands. There is a huge lake that takes your breath away. There are people cycling on cycling tracks it is a wonderful place for cycling. It looks a good place for walking and relaxing. Soon we come to a farm shop which has a camping shop, vegetables for sale, a children's play area and garden shop plus a cafe which is very popular. We have our meal then we drive briskly to Peterborough where we go slightly off track. The sat-nav is guiding us and in addition we use the AA Road Map. We turn round at a farm called Sucarwells, The Three Ducks, it has an equestrian centre and cafe and is open every day. We turn and pass a Union Jack flag. On the way we see someone has put a flag in a side road hedge and it is blowing in the wind.

We arrive at our next bed and breakfast, we refresh ourselves then walk into Peterborough. As we walk across the bridge over the river towards Peterborough there is a Festival of Boats, there are crowds of people on the riverbank side watching. We look and carry on walking into town. We pray and put up our banner in front of a catering establishment that is closed for the day, it is very windy. We wait, as it is a Sunday it is not very busy but people are passing through. We stand for a while, no-one comes to speak, the shops start to close, we put down our banner, as we turn to leave a man comes up with his dog in pup, we give him forty pence and go. We walk to the river and we see a funfair and tents, we find out that this Festival of Boats is supported by Heart Radio Station alongside a newspaper and a local company. There are two great danes who are on leads playing with each other, they have black spots on white fur, they are enjoying themselves. Children are playing, everyone is having a great time. We watch the boats racing. A radio station is giving out music and the weather is fine. We are watching the final races of the boats. There is a group of four boats, the rowers go down the river in their boats, there is a mixture of men and women rowing. A woman goes along in a little speed boat with a loud speaker while another motorised boat waits behind the rowers with people on it. A man stands with his clipboard watching, the four boats go along as they get to the end of the race, unfortunately a boat turns over, the rowers are in the water. The lady in her speed boat goes over to help. The rowers come out wet, as soon as they are out of the river another race is run, then the winners are announced, we decide to go. As we walk along the riverside there is a Swan with her two cygnets, they look like cuddly toys, they are very cute, a photographer comes over and takes a photo. Mum swan makes sure that we do not go too near. We carry on walking and arrive at the bed and breakfast.

Peterborough there is a Festival of Boats

As we think of water we can relate this to the Sea of Galilee, Jesus often went on the Sea of Galilee with his disciples some of whom were fishermen. We can imagine the beautiful sea of Galilee, the men in their fishing boats casting out their nets across the water, the sounds of the birds in the air and the boats full of fish. Galilee was beautiful but the sea could change and turn stormy very quickly, the fishermen were at the weather's mercy. We are told in scriptures Matthew 8:23 how one night Jesus and his disciples were on a boat, Jesus was fast asleep in the boat when a terrible storm came up. As the waves and winds lashed the boat, the disciples grew more and more afraid. Jesus went on sleeping. In the end they woke Him up, He stood up and stilled the water, they realised that Jesus was different, "What kind of man is this?" they asked, "Even the winds and waves obey him," they realised that He was God, not a normal man. Bryn Haworth a Christian singer and musician has written a song entitled 'What Kind Of Man Is This,' expressing Jesus love for us. When we think of the disciples on that boat asking the same question wondering who Jesus was, surely when we go through the storms of life we can call out to Jesus. Gently He will steer our boat into calmer water if only we would let Him. Amen

We travelled 54 miles from Nottingham to Peterborough in Cambridgeshire.

Monday 23 June

Today we leave Peterborough, we are off to Birmingham, we pass through poppy fields which are very pretty, on the radio we heard that they are used for medical purposes. We arrive at our bed and breakfast and refresh ourselves. Wendy, the lady in charge, gives information about the City. We take our leave and walk to the City Centre. We walk round and it is again very busy, people are always stopping you for various things. There are many soldiers here as in York, a man shouts at the soldiers, another man is chased by a policeman down the street. At the end of the main Centre is a statue of Queen Victoria, there is a venue where there are statues and water flowing, this venue was opened by the late Princess Diana in 1993.

As we proceed a man is giving out leaflets. We take one and read it, we realise that he is a Christian. We go back to see him and introduce ourselves. Alan is a 'born again' Christian, comes from Wolverhampton and goes to various town centres to give the Gospel. He comes from the Charismatic Kings Church Ministries. He was prayed over four times by women, wives of church leaders, who confirmed that he would go out and evangelise. Each one not knowing what the other had said. We pray and ask for more Christians to come out on the streets. The more people who come out the more people will ask questions and chat especially if they know that you are committed as far as possible each week, even as a member of a team. In one area of the City there are problems with preaching but this should not deter us to give the Good News where we can. We leave Alan and go down the street. We find a statue of Nelson put up in 1883, there too is a view of St Martins Church.

St Martins Church Birmingham Centre

We pray and find our spot, we put our banner up, it is near a junction, there is a clothes shop and an assortment of shops here. a group of Christian preachers are nearby sharing the Gospel with folk from other faiths and a lady walks through the street singing out loud a hymn. We meet a man called Simon Mason, who is visiting his family from Newport Wales, he has been baptised two weeks ago through Victory Outreach. He told us about a lady called Dinah who has worked in London amongst the homeless and moved to Wales to open a home for them, and also reaching out to prisons for twenty five years. Simon leaves and we meet another Christian named Dave, he comes from Birmingham Baptist Church, he had been a back slidden Christian and had given his life to the Lord on 5 January 1970. A man passes and says "God bless you." Two Pentecostals come up in their late twenties, they are a married couple and chat to us. It was an interesting day. This City is a mass of people composing of Chinese, Japanese, Saudi Arabians, Indians, Pakistanis, all manner of people. Soon it is time to take the banner down and we leave.

From the Victory Outreach we are again reminded of Jesus and Isaiah 61, He went to Galilee and visited His home town Nazareth and read out this piece of scripture in the local synagogue. Jesus came to set the prisoner free, it did not go down well with the people there. They knew Jesus as the child who grew up in Nazareth, his mother was Mary and his father Joseph. By reading out this scripture Jesus was telling the people who he was, God. The people were upset. John the Baptist knew that the signs of the Messiah would be healing. John also knew that people would be baptised with the Holy Spirit and the Spirit of Fire when the Messiah came which we see in the Book of Acts chapter 2. The Holy Spirit came down in tongues of fire and the Apostles spoke in everyone's tongues. Peter spoke to the people, he told them about Jesus dying on the Cross. "Who then can be saved?" they asked. "You can by confessing your sins," Peter answered. Many were saved and baptised that day.

It is not a wonderful thought that no matter how bad we have been we can be forgiven because Jesus died for us. We don't have to be in a prison to be prisoners for we can create our own prison walls, Jesus can break down those walls and set us free with the key of forgiveness amen.

We travelled 85 miles from Peterborough to Birmingham West Midlands.

Wales

Tuesday 24 June

We are off to Aberwysyth in Wales from Birmingham. We pass the Stochen Cross which has a cross as its sign. We pass a Tudor house and we drive along the A44 to Oraohinda where there is a place called Easters Court. Later we go through a village of Tudor houses which are all higgaldy piggaldy, we pass another poppy field and drive onto Llangurig, we are noticing more red colours in the leaves. There are fewer sheep here. There are lots of hedges on the kerb sides of roads. The roads are becoming more and more winding. We see high mountains with trees, we are going towards Wales now. As we pass a field we see donkeys. We look for a place for refreshment, we find a bed and breakfast which does this. There is a dog who was with his master outside, as we get out of the car we speak to the male owner, we find that the dog is commanded by whistles. We go inside and speak to the lady of the house who provides us with refreshments. We feel like we are in a church, it turns out that the bed and breakfast is an ex vicarage which belonged to the local Church called St Curig. We are told that we are in Llangung the centre of Wales, it is the highest village in Wales. 1000 feet above water. This couple have just taken the bed and breakfast over.

Aberwysyth Sea Front

After our refreshments we go to Aberwysyth, we book in and decide to walk into town. As we walk we go for a meal by the sea front. We order lunch, the only problem is the counter is too high for me, the lady serving me gets the giggles and hands the food down as if I am a child. The tables have pigeons flying down, a seagull comes down and stands with his head going up and down, he decides to land on some crockery on a table, he flies up and aims for the table, he misses the table and slides onto the floor. There are many seagulls here on roofs everywhere, they are up early in the morning filling the air with their cries. We leave the cafe and pray for a site to put up the banner. We find a huge plant box and set up our banner there, there are ants walking round the plant wall which are occasionally flicked off us as they tickle. We are standing near a Welsh book shop and at a crossroads with all four roads converging, we wait for people to come, there is a young man near us, he is playing a guitar and singing the Beatles song 'With A Little Help from My Friends,' He then goes off for a break. We are near posters advertising P.J. Proby and other names advertising their music.

Christian Bookshop

Colin goes to the cafe for drinks while Madeleine stays with the banner. Two men come and they joke about the music on the posters. They turn out to be a missionary from India and the local pastor who invites us to a seminar tonight at 7.30 pm in his Church where the Indian missionary is going to speak. They tell us about the Christian Bookshop here. Colin comes back, we both take it in turns to go the shop to find out about its history. We find out that the shop is owned by local churches and run by volunteers, it is interdenominational, we chat to Keith Lewis who is serving. Keith goes to a Welsh speaking church. He tells us about the pastor who had spoken to us. His name is Jeff Thomas who is the pastor of Alfred Place Independent Baptist Church. He tells us about a seminar in August for Christians leaders asking questions about the faith. A photo is taken of the bookshop. The young man comes back with his guitar and continues his music.

We meet a warm friendly Christian lady who has lived in Chester, she is now living in Wales. She found the Lord through ALPHA, that is a Christian course for those who are seeking the faith, she is encouraging people to come to the Lord through ALPHA and they are coming to know the Lord. She has been to Turkey and feels that the Lord is calling her there to work. She is getting married soon. Another man goes past and says "God loves you." We fold up the banner and get ready to go to church in the evening.

Aberwysyth High Street

In the evening we walk to the Church, it is a wet evening. Jeff is waiting at the door and gives us a warm welcome. We sit down as people arrive. We have introductions from Jeff about their newsletter. There are two Dutch Christian ladies who are going back to Holland. We sing a hymn about the 'Blood of Jesus ' and pray. After the prayer we are invited to speak about what we are doing. There are about thirty people of all ages and their faith is strong. Afterwards the missionary, whose name is John from India, comes forward and tells us about his work in India. He speaks about the way women are treated, the outcasts of India, the street children that he and his wife have adopted, about fifty in all, and creationism. The talk is interesting, when the talk finishes we have a chat with the people here. We are told that houses are hard to sell here, there is virtually no selling. Some people do not want houses prices to go down. First time buyers cannot afford them, now there is a stoppage which leads to no chain. Many estate agents are closing down generally in England. We chat to a couple who have been students, they are husband and wife, the wife is from California. They are thinking about outreach and reaching Christians in College, although this is getting harder. We speak to John and we talk about Ken Ham's Course 'Answers in Genesis.' After this, we say good-bye and go out into the rain.

John in his message spoke about the Woman at the Well, as in many parts of the World many women are not treated a equals. Jesus always treated women as equals in a land where they were considered secondary. They had no rights to sell land and if one looks at the story of Ruth, her mother-in-law

Naomi was left with land she could not sell without the aid of a male. As her husband and sons had died she was in dire circumstances, she had to go back to Bethlehem. Ruth went with her, God provides Boaz, a relative to buy Naomi and her land so that he could marry Ruth. If a woman was divorced by her husband she as many others were often left destitute. Jesus had much to say on this and told the Pharisees off. The men could do just as they pleased with their wives. Without male heirs a woman was left in poverty especially if she was without male issue or was childless. Woman who were made pregnant by a male were stoned, and still are today in some cultures, even if she is raped. Two witnesses are brought against her to say that she consented. This is why when we read the Christmas Story, Mary the mother of Jesus is told by the Angel Gabriel that she will have a son by the Holy Spirit. Joseph, her husband to be, does not know about this and decides to end the engagement quietly because he does not want Mary stoned. However he has a dream, in this dream the angel tells him that Mary has been made pregnant by the Holy Spirit , Joseph changes his mind and he decides to bring up Jesus as his own child and marry Mary. As time goes by Jesus grows up, people have heard stories about Him, indeed the Pharisees make accusations about Him as half Samaritan, and what sort of woman was his mother. We can only imagine how He felt and his mother by the insults that they had slung at them. Many times He was asked "Who is your Father?" but He continued to trust His Heavenly Father, he continued to do His Father's work. He prayed, told people stories, His Father was His strength. He has given us the Lord's Prayer so that we know who and where His Father is, "Our Father who art in Heaven." we too can trust in our Lord Jesus Christ and when we say this prayer we are brothers and sisters in Christ, trusting in Him every day for unlike our earthly father, He will never let us down.

We travelled 85 miles from Birmingham to Aberwsyth in west Wales.

Wednesday 25 June

Today we travel form Aberwysyth to Camarthen, we notice again many hedges on the grass verges. We see sheep by the sea, the colourful houses. Again there winding roads. Another difference here too is instead of hedges separating the fields there is fencing going all the way round, the sheep are black headed. We pass donkeys, cows, black hens. We stop and ask a local postie for a cafe, he is very friendly and helpful. We find the cafe he has mentioned but it has closed down, next door there is a shop where you can buy food and refreshments, it is also a petrol station. The rain is coming down, there are Union Jacks and Welsh flags flying. The wind too is strong. We have a look at the view it is amazing, the river winds its way round, there are black, black and white mixed colour cows in the distance and a pretty bridge. There are hills all around. We meet two farmers, a husband and wife whose cows are in the distance. They work all day with them, the cows are out in the summer, all day and night. In the winter or when they are calving they have sheds to dwell in. The farmers go out in the morning and they end their day at about 5 o'clock, feeding them. They do not have names for them but they know their cows as each has a personality. They have about 300.

Travelling to Camarthen

After we finish speaking to the farmers we go into the shop, we speak to a Welsh young lady, she has lived in Wales all her life, she has a Welsh hat from her childhood where they celebrate St David's day at school. We have our meal in the car and drive to the next bed and breakfast, we book in and tidy up, we are on our way to Camarthen.

We take the car and pass through the town, it is busy. We park in a car park which also houses a doctors surgery and pharmacy. There is payment for long and short stays. The colour pink is painted on short stay parking and white for normal stay. After sorting out the parking we go down a little side road where there is washing in the small front garden as we pass. We pray for a spot in the centre. We find the place to put our banner and go and have a meal in the local British Home Store. We walk back to town and set up our banner in the market square. This is a place where people sit and a Bakers Oven, the market stalls are spread across the market square in bright colours.

Across the way there is a van selling all of manner of food and teas, a man appears opposite us with his black dog. The dog has a collar and a huge pink scarf going into a bow. The man has a pram frame, it has four wheels and a chair with a case, a bag in with a blanket and a dog bowl are installed inside. He pulls out the the chair, he then spreads a blanket out for his dog, the pram is left on the side. There is a bottle of water for the dog which is placed under the blanket. The dog bowl is taken out and filled for the dog to drink which he does. The dog is very interested across the way as the tea van has smells of meat cooking, he lifts his nose longingly up towards the van. The man takes out of his case an accordion, after this a board with a message is put out, he goes for a tea and comes back to play. The dog gets hot, an umbrella comes forth, it is tied onto the pram to shade him. The music begins, it is a blend of songs of the past of songs in the war and songs from the musicals, it is very well done.

Camarthen Castle

The afternoon progresses, people sit drinking and resting from shopping. There is also a couple, a man and wife selling photo poems to children's names. They feed the pigeons while they are there. A romantic song floats from the accordion and two pigeons start canoodling to the music, it looks very comical. The couple selling cards decide to leave early. A Christian lady comes along, she has lived in Camarthen all her life, her son is a pastor of an Evangelical Church in Pembrokeshire. He was brought up in a Christian home and gave his life to the Lord at eighteen years of age. This lady mentioned that there was a summer conference each year in August, everyone is welcome, it was the same summer conference as Keith in the Christian bookshop in Aberwysyth had mentioned. She tells us that there is a Christian book shop here. After we finish speaking Colin goes to find the bookshop. We find out that the bookshop is run by a husband and wife team, they are called Albert and Beth Haynes, they have run this in Camarthen for the past twenty five years since 1981. Albert gave up his secular job to help run a stall with his wife. Albert and Beth know Pastor Jeff of the Alfred Place Independent Baptist Church in Aberwysyth. We meet a Christian man who belongs to a small church in the area.

We chat to the man playing the accordion, he can read music, he plays many instruments, he has been in places where we have been on the Journey and he has played in Hounslow High Street, west London, near to where we live. He has seen Holy Trinity Church and Hounslow Christian Community Church. He has a travelling van.

Camarthen Shopping Centre

At 5 o'clock we pack up the banner, we travel back to the bed and breakfast, outside our window we have a view of the fields, the grass is being gathered in bales. A tractor cuts the grass into rows. Then a plough was put onto a tractor and taken round to fluff up the grass to make it thicker. Then another tractor comes, the grass is scooped up into the machine at the back of the tractor and it opens in half and a roll was deposited. Another machine comes and lifts the hay onto another machine, a person puts on a black plastic strip, The bale roll turns round and round the plastic envelopes the roll. When the roll is covered, the machine tips the bale off. A worker comes and rolls it away.

When we think of the harvest, the story of Ruth and Naomi comes to mind, Naomi sadly loses her husband Elimelech and her two sons Mahlon and Kilion die leaving no grandsons. Naomi had travelled with her husband and two young sons from Bethlehem to Moab as there was a famine in Bethlehem at that time. Naomi's sons grow up and marry two women called Orpah and Ruth. When all three men die, Naomi decides to take Ruth and Orpah to their families to marry someone else. Orpah goes back to her family, Ruth decides to travel with Naomi to Bethlehem. Ruth decides to follow Yahweh the God of Naomi. The women have no food, Ruth decides to pick up the gleanings from the fields to make bread. God had instructed the Israelites to leave some barley and wheat on the sides of the fields for the poor to take. She meets Boaz, who owns the field, who is related to Naomi, he is impressed by Ruth's kindness to her mother-in-law Naomi. Boaz a man of faith marries Ruth who is a gentile, non Jew woman, who marries into the Israel nation, through Ruth's

105

faith comes the line of Jesse, King David and the promised one, the Messianic line. The Messiah being Jesus. Through one woman's courageous faith Ruth, to another Mary, accepting to carry the Son of God. Jesus, spoke of the Harvest, He Himself was the Bread. The Bread of Life. "Feed on me and you will never be hungry." Thus God provided Manna, a form of bread for the Israelites travelling to the Promised Land, to Ruth gathering the wheat and the barley to make bread, to Mary who delivered the Bread of Life, Jesus. Jesus himself declared "I am the Bread of Life. He who comes to me will never go hungry, and he who believes in Me will never be thirsty." John 6 :35. Eat of Jesus and feast on Him, you will never regret it.

We travelled 80 miles from Aberwysyth to Camarthen.

26 June Thursday

We are to travel from Camarthen to Cardiff, today we go for an early morning walk in the countryside, there is a river flowing past the garden of the bed and breakfast. We meet a neighbour who is walking his dog, he knows Hounslow, Kew Gardens, he has a daughter who lives in Kew. The fields have been cleared of bales which have been piled high in a yard. We see a farmers cat sitting looking at us on the wall, there is a farmers wife busy working on the farm. We then walk back to the bed and breakfast. There are House Martins here, they are feeding their babies, they swoop around. There are Red Kites here too although we have never seen them. The house has two cats who have their own shed. We have breakfast and set off to Cardiff.

We are amused by a sign on an inn as we pass saying 'Open for lunch usually.' We go onto the M4 to Cardiff, we pass the Swansea area where there was the 1904 Welsh Revival led by a young man named Evan Robert's who lived at Langhoer. The houses are as colourful as Scotland. As we progress the land is becoming more built up. We stop at a cafe with a W H Smiths, the weather is hot. We continue our journey and arrive at the next bed and breakfast, we go upstairs to our room where we have a view from our window of a garden with a palm tree and apple tree which has grown into it. We leave our room and walk into the City. There is Cardiff Castle with pictures of soldiers on its walls. Opposite is a Victorian Arcade with little cafes and shops, it is a little bit like Windsor Surrey which has an arcade, only wider. We go into the arcade and have a meal in a Italian cafe devoted to musicians like Mozart, Bach, Handel etc., the meals are done to the themes of their music, the chef is an Italian man.

Cardiff Castle

We finish our meal, we go into the High Street and pray for a spot. We went up and down and we duly find one. We are near a road with work being processed. To our left Marks & Spencers is being refurbished. We unfold our banner and wait. We pray for Christians and non Christians to speak to us. Our prayers are answered when a Christian man named Iminos comes to speak to us, he stays with us for most of the afternoon. He comes from South Africa, he has lived in New York, Cornwall and London. We are able to speak about places we know. He has been to the City Temple Church in Cardiff. He tells us about 'Teen Challenge' and of a healing of a man connected with them. 'Teen Challenge' comes from the ministry of David Wilkinson, well known for the book and film 'Cross and Switchblade' that depicts gang warfare in New York and the subsequent Christian conversion of Nicky Cruise. Pat Boone, a Christian himself, played David Wilkinson in the film. Nicky now goes all over the world telling people about Jesus and how his life has changed. David tells Nicky that Jesus Loved Him. Nicky's life starts to change after being told this. It is a testimony of how one man David Wilkinson went forth into unknown territory into teenage gangs who were violent and were not afraid to use knives. David went into the ghettos of New York to reach these youngsters.

We need more of these people today. People need to know that Jesus loves them. It is a hurting World that is lost. A World that is hungry for the love of God, a reason for living and wants answers which we can give. We are not all called to speak to people on the streets but it could be our neighbour, the young person going down the road, all manner of people. We should have the boldness to speak out, tell them of the love of Jesus. A person could be saved through your boldness and many others, just as David told Nicky of Jesus' Love for him, Nicky now tells others. They are still doing this today, therefore go forth and multiply, tell others today.

A man from Portugal comes up, his name is Emmanuel, his English is limited, he points to the sign at the Commandment number four. 'Remember to keep the Sabbath Day, to keep it Holy." We speak a little to him although he speaks little English. We use gestures and signs, he tells us that in Portugal that their Sabbath is on a Saturday. Emmanuel does jobs and he is a cleaner. There are thousands of people passing the banner, a little boy comes up and points out Wales to his mother on our map.

Cardiff Shopping Centre

A man is singing dressed as a Jester, he has a Jesters hat with red trousers and top, he went up and sang to people, they are laughing. He is certainly a colourful character. At 6 o'clock we fold up the banner, the wind is blowing and it is raining. We say good-bye to Emmanuel. We see as we go pass that the Jester is still singing in a shop doorway. We pass a dog, he is very friendly and we make a fuss of him and go on our way.

Cardiff is an interesting City, there are loads of CCTV cameras. By the bed and breakfast there is a river and a stadium. In the bed and breakfast we hear the news about the windmills. We have nicknamed them armies, from the description of a man in Stornoway, "they are like arms flying around," he said. We have seen many on the hillsides blowing around in the wind, from Scotland almost to Wales. People do not seem to like them, perhaps they may be better in a green colour, perhaps someone from government should have asked people what design and colour they would like to blend in with their countryside.

Thinking about telling people about Jesus, two songs come to mind, 'Go tell everyone, the wonderful things that God has done' and 'Colours of Day,' telling us to go out and tell us the Good News of Jesus. Jesus went out to the highways and byways to tell the people about Himself, Zaccheus was a tax collector, he was a small man and wanted to see Jesus. Zaccheus was like a lot of tax collectors in those days, he pocketed some of the money for himself and gave the rest to the Romans who were in charge of Israel. People hated the tax collectors for this. Zaccheus heard that Jesus was visiting town so he shinned up a tree. He waited patiently, Jesus saw him, he called to Zaccheus up the tree. "Zaccheus come on down, I am having a meal in your place today." Zaccheus came down and took Jesus to his home. Zaccheus changed during that visit and offered to give half the money back that he had taken. What joy was in that household. Jesus showed Zaccheus love and he responded. The Pharisees and Sadducees would not reach these people or tell them of the God's love for them. Instead they had become religious and sadly thought that they were above everyone else. Jesus on many occasions was upset at their attitude because they did not like Him mixing with the tax collectors or anyone else for that matter, Jesus having dinner at Zaccheus house with His friends, the Pharisees were annoyed and wondered why Jesus wanted to eat with these people. He had came to heal the sick not the healthy, as he told them. We are all fallen people from God from the time of Adam and Eve. Ever since Eve took the apple tempted by Satan. Sin came in and the the world has been corrupted ever since. The first son of Adam and Eve, Cain, killed his brother Abel whose blood was spilt on the ground. The first animal died to clothe Adam and Eve when they sinned. Animals were sacrificed from that time especially lambs, until the second Adam came to redeem the first Adam's fall by dying on the Cross for all man's sin and now animals do not need to be sacrificed again. Jesus has undone the damage Satan did in the Garden of Eden. "And he will crush your head", we are told in Genesis 3: 15. Yahweh God was speaking of the future Messiah who would crush and defeat Satan by being victorious on the Cross. Jesus' birth and death has been done, He has risen from the dead. All we need to do is accept Him as our Saviour taking us away from the jaw's of Satan from the kingdom of darkness into the Kingdom of Light. Amen

We travelled 75 miles from Camarthen to Cardiff in South Wales.

England

27 June Friday

Today we travel to Bristol from Cardiff. As we travel the towns are turning back into countryside. There are trees, bridges, and rivers. We see a sign for Monmouthshire, there is a small church on a farm surrounded by barns, byres and cows, it is an unusual sight to see. It is probably one of the first churches built in England by the early Christian Church. When Christianity came over to England Churches were built on farmland and people worshipped in them from the surrounding area. They are small compared to today's church buildings. Today they are owned by the Church of England, the farmer/landlord has duties and maintains the church building being on his land and pays for this, he also has the right to insist that a son of his can become a vicar and run the church for the rest of his life.

In this area there are more cows, they are mainly black or a mixture of black and white. What you do notice as you progress down from Scotland is that the cows are not so varied in colour as in England. On some farms also the sheep go from pure white to apricot, chocolate, into black. We have seen quite a few black sheep whereas in Surrey and London you would very occasionally see a black sheep, sometimes they may have black heads but that is as far as the colouring will go. We soon reach the Seventh Bridge, a sign comes forth 'Welcome to England in English and Welsh. Bristol is a big city, as in Yorkshire there are steep roads with houses going downhill. There is a road called High Street and not for nothing is this called this. There is also a Zoo here and gardens. The sat-nav guides us to the bed and breakfast in addition to checking signs and AA road maps.

We arrive at the bed and breakfast where we sign in, then we make our way to the City. We find a restaurant which is called Extra Plus. They use Fairtrade food and their profits go into a charity called Tenorvous Trust for cancer. After our meal we take a bus into the city. There are many shops as we travel along and there is a Wesley Owen Christian Bookshop.

We get off the bus and cross the road. To our amazement we are outside the first Wesleyian Church, the oldest Methodist building in the world. We look and walk inside, there is a small garden, in front is the statue of John Wesley.

We enter the Church doors, as it is a Friday there has been a communion which is 1 o'clock every Friday. John Wesley's Chapel is also called the New Room that dates back to 1739. Today it is a place of worship and pilgrimage around the world. This was John Wesley's first headquarters from where he travelled all over the country, "Preaching the glad tidings of Salvation."

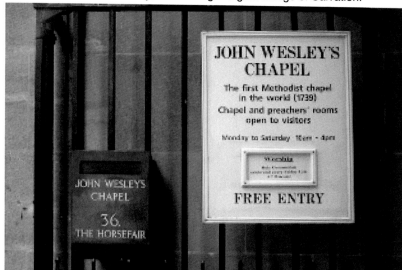

In the United States of America is John Street, New York City, which has the oldest Methodist site in America. As you go in there is a buzz of people chatting. All the original pews are there. On your left side is history about John Wesley and the English and American Church. You walk to the end of the Church and there are stairs on your left leading to the balcony. You climb up the stairs and walk across the balcony with the pews. There is a painting of the congregation of yesteryear listening to the preaching. You come to the end of the balcony, you turn right and go up more stairs eventually you reach the preachers room which divides into two. One part, as you go through to your right, is a table and chairs where the elders had their meetings. You turn left and there is another room which has a dividing wall which slides backwards and forwards, by this divide is a bed showing where John Wesley slept, in the makeshift doorway to your right is the window facing the moors. John Wesley wrote his sermons standing up on the window sill looking out on the view, the floor has a wooden ledge where he put his feet, the panel still bears his footprints to this day. Facing you in the doorway is a glass cabinet with a dummy clothed in John Wesley's vestments. We leave this room and turn right where there is a bookshop and a couple of volunteers are there, a man and a woman. She then takes us back to the bedroom and demonstrates to us where the saying 'sleep tight' comes from. She explains, in those days beds were done with ropes rather than strings, the ropes went through holes at the bottom of the bed and these would be tightened to the bedstead, hence 'sleep tight.' We chat a few minutes more. Adjoining is the house of Charles Wesley, the brother of John Wesley, where Charles wrote hymns and people can arrange to see this house. Groups and schools can visit. The New Chapel is open, except Sundays. This is run by volunteers and donations are gratefully accepted.

Statue of John Wesley outside the Chapel

We leave the building having enjoyed a quick visit knowing that it was the Hand of God leading us there. It was encouraging to see how one person's faith could lead to so much and how another used his gift of hymn writing, whose hymns we sing today. The Wesley brothers' parents were Susanna and Samuel Wesley who were a man and woman of great faith, their children were brought up in this faith. Samuel himself was a preacher in the church, from these parents were to come children who in their turn would have the faith. It was a thrill for a few minutes to be a part of that past of John Wesley, a new church beginning, a preaching started and many were saved.

Inside John Wesley's Chapel

We have in our family tree an ancestor who was 'born again'. His parents were Christians. His mother was a Wesleyian, probably one of the first Wesleylians in Lincolnshire. It is exciting to see, from John Wesley's preaching, two generations of people finding the Lord. John Wesley actually preached at a place called 'The Stump' in Boston Lincolnshire. A man called Selwyn Hughes, best known for 'Every day with Jesus' publication, was a second generation man who became a Christian. He was a young man who saw his uncle saved by the Welsh Revival of Evan Roberts in 1949.

We go back into the sunshine and we set off to the High Street to give 'the Glad Tidings of Salvation,' to the present day people. When John Wesley preached the 'Good News' the Industrial Revolution had arrived, people had moved from the countryside to the factories, it was a time of upheaval for them for their homes on the land had gone. They had lived for generations on the land and now faced machines and brick walls in exchange for the open air. Today there is, as in other cities, a mixture of faiths and cultures, there is a new generation to reach. People have come from other countries into a new land which is not their own. So the Gospel needs to be shared with these people as John Wesley did all those years ago with the country people moving into factories. Today people need to be reached with the Gospel, we need the John Wesley's of today to go out, 'preaching the glad tidings of Salvation' so that one generation can tell another.

We pray looking for a spot, as we walk round we notice as with other cities there is regeneration on the way with pavements, roads, shops being refurbished. We find a spot in a market square near a departmental store which is near a tea stall. We pray again, the banner is raised. A lady comes along, she says that she is spiritual. She had been in the Girls Brigade and had received from them a Bible. She belongs to a church but has been unable to go because of her work shifts. She has not been to church since she joined, she is reading things up and would like to travel the world. She takes a leaflet and moves on. A second older lady comes to speak, she comes from St Andrews, Scotland, she is a Christian and is a Methodist.

A man comes along to speak, his name is Martin and works in the media, he is still seeking spiritual answers. He takes two leaflets asking questions. Joseph follows, he is a bit the worse for wear, he comes from Ireland and is now living in Bristol. He says that he is drunk, he normally drives a truck, today he is too drunk to drive it. "How can God love a drunk?" he asks, we chat for a while. He asked if we knew where he could go for Christian help. We explain that we do not live in the area, we give him a leaflet, he goes off quite happy, we pray that he will find the help he needs.

It is a nice afternoon meeting people. Soon it is time to leave, we pack up our banner and go back to the bed and breakfast. So many people like Joseph do need to know that Jesus loves them. Nicky Cruise came to the Lord by David Wilkerson telling him that Jesus loves him. David never gave up telling Nicky this and through David's persistence Nicky came to know Jesus and then consequently thousands through the witness of Nicky. We need to keep on telling people that Jesus loves them, and to believe in Him. We must reach every one with the Good News of the Lord Jesus Christ.

Jesus spoke to the Samaritan woman at Jacob's well. The disciples had gone shopping for bread from a nearby house. The woman was drawing water from the well and chatted to Jesus, as she did so Jesus told her that she had had many husbands in her life and the man she has now was living with her. This lady knew that there was something different about Jesus, she was lost and knew that her life was wrong but had continued to live that way, she believed that a Messiah was to come. She then recognised that Messiah was Jesus who was standing before her, she saw what the Pharisees and Sadducees refused to see. When Jesus spoke to her about her husbands she left her pitcher and ran to the village and told all the people there, she brought them to Jesus. By this time the disciples had returned, they were all invited to the village, they went to the village and they chatted to the people. Many people gave their lives to God and believed in Jesus. John 4.

God desires that we turn our lives to Him through Christ and to tell others. This can be done in everyday conversation and in what we do. Jesus did not do anything spectacular, instead He sat down the well and chatted to a lady. She was interested. He did not say, "You are an adulteress." He told her she had five husbands, she was intrigued and ran to tell the people in the town. "Could this be the Messiah." she asks. The men came out following a women who was living with different men but God had revealed to her who Jesus was. He tried through the so called righteous people who would not listen but the 'sinners' did. Many came that day to the Lord. Will you pray for the prostitute down the road, the drunkards, the homeless, a drug addicted parent, a parent who has been left single, the sick. Tell people today, you never know, your whole street could turn to the Lord.

We travelled 44 miles from Cardiff to Bristol.

28 June Saturday

Today we travel from Bristol to Worcester, we have an upstairs view of the park from the window of our bed and breakfast, today it is full of activity. We have seen a classic car go across the park with two male drivers, people running, people walking dogs and people cycling, the scene at night was very pretty with a 'castle like' building lit up.

There is also here the history of the Parliamentarians and Prince Rupert leading the Cavaliers. Prince Rupert, nephew of Charles 1 and a good military man decided to take on the Parliamentarians from here, Rupert had an army. The Parliamentarians agreed and met Prince Rupert and his army here, they had a battle, Prince Rupert fought and burnt down part of Cliften Bridge, in the end he was defeated. He and his soldiers were allowed to retreat. England was in a civil battle between the Roundheads who were Puritans fighting alongside the Parliamentarians led by Oliver Cromwell against the Cavaliers, supporters of Charles 1. It was a battle of the King against Parliament claiming 'The Divine Right of Kings' which in the end cost Charles 1 his life. This was to be a bone of contention, even in Charles II's time when he came back from exile in France, to claim the throne after Oliver Cromwell died as by this time England had become a Republic. The purification of the Church had come in and this movement has remained in some form in the Christian Church ever since. Oliver Cromwell and his troops went through many churches destroying anything that had the flavour of the Church of Rome. When Cromwell took over England he made man and woman wear black clothes. The women wore white caps over their hair and white aprons. Men wore black hats, dancing was frowned upon. On Christmas day churches were not allowed to open so no-one could celebrate Christmas day in their churches. This changed when Charles II came onto the English throne, much to the people's relief.

We drive out of Bristol and we are onto the motorway with the sat-nav giving instructions. We stop at a motorway and have a short walk. Soon after we arrive in Worcester and go to our bed and breakfast. After booking in we walk towards the Centre. We find a cafeteria called Judith's cafe, we have a meal and carry on walking, we pass a blind lady with her back guide dog. The first building you notice is a Cathedral, today there is a wedding with Rolls Royce's, there are lots of men dressed in cravat style and ladies wearing fashionable small hats with nets.

Worcester

As you walk into the Centre, in front of the cathedral it is like a square, opposite the buses and cars go past. We walk towards the shopping precinct, there are small alleyways passing from the main streets. We pass a shop called Madeleine Ann on our left and an old County Hall with a Queen Ann statue in the centre of the wall. There are paintings posted all over the railings for people to see.

As we go along the Guide dogs for the Blind are collecting money. There are guide dogs sitting, and a guide dog in training with its trainer. The People's Friend magazine too has been doing a series on a guide dog called Faye, from her puppy hood to her adulthood in training. It is wonderful to see that God has given the gift of dogs to help us and we are now seeing hearing dogs with their owners wearing their blue coats. Dogs are a blessing to us in many ways. As pets, companions, police dogs, friends. There is a Christian singer called Marilyn Baker, Marilyn is blind, she has a guide dog called Penny who helps her in her work. Marilyn has written many Christian songs, perhaps the best known is "You are the Potter and I am the Clay." Marilyn also plays the piano, she has been blind since birth. Jesus has used Marilyn to bring His love to others and to share the Good News. She has a special ministry to people who are disabled. Her songs are Jesus inspired. Marilyn has a assistant called Tracy who too is a gifted woman in her own right, together they use their gifts to express the love of Jesus through music, prophetic and dance.

Worcester County Hall

Worcester Shopping Centre

We carry on walking praying for a spot to put our banner. God answers our prayer, we set it up against a wall opposite Marks and Spencers. As we stand there the Mayor walks pass, following him are some young women are giving out leaflets for New Age healing, life changes. They are about fifteen years of age, one has a belt with the words 'Jesus Loves You.' We are approached by two men, they come to chat, they are from the Unitarian Church. They like the banner and say that it is good. They comment that schools should have the Ten Commandments. They agree with the scripture but not that Jesus is God. They think that we are brave to do what we are doing. They leave and a lady comes along from a local church. She does not know Jesus, she has not had a clear teaching from her church, she is very mixed up. She takes a leaflet and goes. We then meet Tim whom Jesus is clearly speaking to. He had asked Jesus to let him know if He existed. He has had a vision of Heaven and

Hell. Jesus is asking him to accept Jesus as his Saviour in his life and the immersion of the Holy Spirit. We explain the scripture to him and Acts 2, he is pleased about this and wonders why there is not more teaching. We suggest that he buys copies of Jill Briscoe's books and tapes in the local Christian bookshop. We do suggest Christian radio but a lot of people have radios and cannot get Christian radio as they are outside the transmission area. They do not have internet facilities to hear them. We advise him to find a church teaching about Jesus and being 'born again'.

Tim leaves and we meet Keith from America who now lives in Kidderminster. He cannot find a church that suits him. He likes meeting people. Some churches are a bit religious but not Spirit filled, he tells us. Keith leaves and another man comes up. He originates form Ealing, Norwood Green. He goes to a church in Worcester, he listens to loads of Christian radio. He seems to be mixed up as so many people seem to be, people do not know what they believe in. People come up and look, another man called Peter comes along, he has been in the army. He is a single man having been married, he has found the Lord. He is a volunteer in a Christian bookshop and is keen to tell people about Jesus, he goes fo a local church. He introduces us to his friend Emma and leaves. A Chinese man comes up, he is a Christian student at university studying business, he takes a photo and leaflet. It is an incredible afternoon meeting these people. We are told that two preachers do come and preach at each end of the town on a Saturday but people throw things at them.

We see two men come along with paint buckets upside down, they sit and bang them with one rhythm and then go. A band plays at the other end of Centre in the street market with the mayor. The paintings are being put away, one falls and breaks, the guide dogs start to go. We notice as in other places, a new group of people start to come, normally families shopping with younger people. As time passes older teens start to come in. One young man is wearing a T-shirt, the word destruction and a skull are printed on it and there are words in Welsh. Another man is wearing a T shirt, on his T shirt are the words, 'God can't wait,' underneath these words is the face of the devil with the words, 'he can.' At 5 o'clock we pack up the banner and we walk back to the bed and breakfast.

As we reflect on the afternoon we are reminded of Nicodemus who went to Jesus at night. Nichodemus was a Pharisee and member of the Jewish ruling council, it was preferable to speak to Jesus by night as the religious rulers would not be pleased. Nicodemus knew that Jesus was different, he recognised that the healings Jesus performed came from God. Jesus spoke to him about about being 'born again'. Nicodemus was puzzled, to him birth was when a baby comes out of a mother's womb and that was only once, you cannot go back into the womb and come out again. Jesus explains that when we are born it is a birth of the flesh. A human baby is formed in a human being, when we find Jesus, we are as a spiritual baby being born into a new spiritual life, we change and do not want our old flesh life back, we have entered God's

Kingdom here on earth and for ever. So many people in this country do not know Jesus personally, sadly even sometimes those who go to church. Our late vicar, John Barter, was criticised for saying 'you must be born again' in his sermons. His answer was that people must be saved, some people do not know Jesus as their Saviour even when they go to church, he would continue to give people this message. Nicodemus became a believer. We must explain this to people and give them proper teaching, it is then up to them to decide. It is important to speak to others and to debate, for people to have time to listen, to hear preaching and to listen to teaching. It is no good having people continually coming to church and to have no faith, they need to believe. As Jesus said to Nichodemus, "You must be born again."

We travelled 62 miles from Bristol to Worcester

29 June Sunday

Today we travel to Oxford, we say good-bye to Worcester. We travel onwards towards the motorway, there is a tractor on the fields with seagulls in the sky flying around. Today we notice that a field where there is normally red soil a harvest is coming through. On a grass verge is a baby bunny. The sat-nav seems a bit confused, on the grass verges there are red poppies looking very pretty. There are scarecrows in the field and a golf course. As we travel through the countryside to the Chilterns the weather is getting warmer. London according to the news is the hottest place. We see a beautiful hill with a castle and trees.

Worcester to Oxford

The Church is called the Parish Church of St Laurence. We carry on driving, the market town goes into a more modern street. We pass a fire station which is the centre of 'Fire Training' in England. There is an area called 'Even Lode' which is two miles away. We continue our journey and pass Blenheim Palace where Winston Churchill was born in Woodstock. We pass on the road a broken down classic car heading for Brighton.

St Mary the Virgin Oxford where John and Charles Wesley preached

We arrive at the bed and breakfast, we book in and walk to Oxford. We look round and pray for a spot to put up our banner, we walk to the University Church of St Mary the Virgin where John and Charles Wesley preached and where the Oxford movement began and where Latimer, Ridley and Cranmer were burnt to death by Queen Mary for their part in the Protestant movement. There are groups of people with guides especially American and young children. Mary was the daughter of King Henry VIII and Catherine of Aragon. Catherine was a fervent Catholic.

She was married to Henry's older brother Arthur at thirteen years of age, Prince Arthur died at fifteen years of age. She married his brother Prince Henry, this was to cause divorce between her and Henry was to fall out with the Pope over this marriage because Catherine could not produce the desired son Henry wanted, although they had a daughter called Mary. Henry VIII thought about this, he looked in the Bible and he came up with Leviticus chapter 18:16 which states, 'Do not have sexual relations with your brother's wife, that would dishonour you', and chapter 20:21 which states, 'If a man marries his brothers wife, it is an act of impurity, he has dishonoured his brother. They will be childless.' Henry VIII used these scriptures in his argument with the Pope.

The Church in England was to split into the Roman Catholic Church which kept the Pope as its head and the Protestant Church of England which was to have an archbishop. Time moved on, Henry VIII died, the throne passed to his Protestant son Edward VI who dies young, the throne eventually going to his eldest daughter, Princess Mary. Mary tried to make England a Catholic country again, she married King Philip of Spain an ardent Catholic and had English Protestants burnt. In time Princess Elizabeth, a Protestant, ascends to the throne after her sister Queen Mary's I death. Queen Elizabeth allowed the Protestants and Catholics to live in relative peace and the freedom to worship in either type of church. She too was a victim of her half sister Mary who kept her prisoner in the Tower of London.

As we walk into the High Street we look for the place where Latimer, Ridley and Cranmer were burnt for their faith. On asking a passer by, who was a priest, he indicated that the original site located in the centre of the road had been removed leaving a small cross and a plaque erected on the wall nearby. It was most disappointing, no-one seems to know much about it when we asked where it happened. We live in a day and age where we have a choice to be Catholic or Protestant. Bishop Hugh Latimer died because he helped established the Anglican Church of England. Bishop Nicholas Ridley for the same reason. They were burnt together in Oxford in 1555 for heresy by Queen Mary. Archbishop Thomas Cranmer was the man who helped Henry VIII with three of his divorces, he as John Knox was keen that people should be able to read the Bible in their own language, he had an English Bible put in every church. He produced the Book of Common Prayer which John Knox helped him to produce in the reign of King Edward VI.

John Knox himself had to flee to Geneva which was a Protestant stronghold where he was to meet John Calvin from whom Calvinism came in the Protestant Church. John Knox was to go back to Scotland and fight against Mary Queen of Scots.

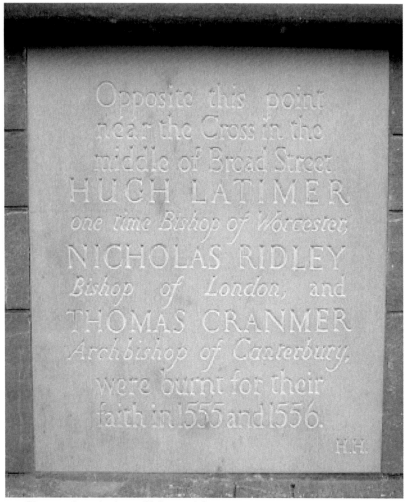

Plaque where Latimer, Ridley and Cranmer were martyred for their faith

We see a TV crew filming a person with a group of people watching in the distance. In the High Street there is an old Saxon tower. There is also a plaque about the Queen's Oxford Hussars who started as Yeomanry. There is a street that is named the Cornmarket from the days of corn sold here. There is also a street called Ship Street which has Tudor buildings. We pray and put our banner up in front of a shop called Gap. The High Street is teeming with people going up and down. Not many people are looking or asking questions. There seems to be apathy. A piper plays in the distance, he is playing many

Scottish songs. He is a man in his early thirties with hair down to his waist, in pony tail style. A lady near us is playing the guitar. Two men, one is dressed as a bear, walks up and down with a bucket. We are near two coin telephone boxes, a man keeps coming round and checking to see if anyone has left any change in the telephone dish. Two men come up to us and ask us if we have any change. We have some grapes, a little girl whose mum has given her an ice cream cone decides that the grapes are more interesting than her ice cream, her mum pulls her away.

Church where John Wesley preached

It does seem sometimes that people are more interested in the supernatural than God, as there are Ghost Tours here, than accepting Jesus as their Saviour. We are more prepared to believe in haunted houses and ghostly stories than reading the Bible and believing in a supernatural God. We can have sadly a museum Christianity. People can go to church and say that's nice, the sermon is nice, the scripture is good, chat and have a cup of tea and then go home. People may ask, 'are you a Christian' and often we answer "yes" and that's it. We often have our 'museum faith' taking Jesus out of the cabinet and then placing Him back again when we are finished with Him. Jesus is not an exhibit, He is living. He does not want to be in a cabinet and looked at. He wants to be part of our lives, take Him out of the museum and see Him as our Living God.

St Mary the Virgin Oxford

The people in the High Street see Christianity as a dead religion, having no relevance to them. The shops have their goods displayed very colourfully, sales posters inviting people to buy cheaper goods. They meet friends, have coffee, there is no need of God. They by-pass God. The tills tinkle with money. The people's bags get bigger. Their faith gets smaller, He is a museum piece in glass cabinet, to them. A man goes past with his friend, he asks his friend if he has been 'born again'. 'Jesus loves you' was read loudly about twice by passers by, people looked but very little compared to the other cities. Two men again pass with painted T shirts, one man has a picture of a skull the other has one his T shirt the skull and crossbones signifying death. We end at 5 o'clock, we pass a fifteen year old lad playing the saxophone, he plays it well.

As we think about the afternoon, we are reminded of the story of the young man who went to Jesus in Mark's Gospel Chapter 10:17. The young man who had great wealth went to see Jesus and asked Jesus what he needed to do to inherit eternal life. He called Jesus, 'Good.' Jesus tells him that only God is Good. Jesus goes through some of the the Ten Commandments with the young man. The young man explains that he has kept the Commandments since a child. Jesus we are told looked at this man with love. He then tested the young man by asking him to give up his wealth and follow Him and he would then have treasures in Heaven. The young man is sorrowful. He could not do this, his wealth came first. This young man had a museum faith, it was good to look at, he was dutiful but when it came to it, he preferred his way of life and the wealth he had gained. His wealth came before his faith. Just as some people like shopping before belief, take away the shops, they would be lost.

As in the days of Noah, they will be eating, drinking, marrying, giving in marriage. Matthew 24:38, Are we also in a museum faith looking at our exhibits, could we give something back like telling someone about our faith. Can we do this today no-matter how big or small. Can we be like the rich young man dutifully doing our bit, but when Jesus asks us to go the extra mile we turn away as we need our comfort, just as those people need their shops. Can we not go out to these people and give them the Good News and say as Jesus said, "Come follow me."

We travelled 58 miles from Worcester to Oxford.

30 June Monday

Today we say good-bye to Oxford, we have a lovely chat with our hostess of the bed and breakfast, she originates from Scotland, we chat about the places in Scotland we visited. There are allotments opposite our room. People are busy on them. There are three flags, two St George's and one for England, probably Rugby. After our chat we are on our way to Luton. We go along the M1 on which the roads are being widened. We see a workman busy in a wheelbarrow. He is kneeling as if he is cooking in it, so intent is he on what he is doing. We arrive early in Luton. The owner of the bed and breakfast allows us in. He helps us with our luggage and makes us a cup of tea, we sit and wait in his garden while our room is being made ready. Roy and his wife Dorothy used to live in St. Albans Herts until they moved to Luton.

When our room is ready we change and walk to the High Street, as we walk along we see a very lively Luton Charismatic Church Church with a phone number written above the door. We introduce ourselves by a phone call and after the conversation we take a photo of the building.

Luton Pentecostal Church

We walk on and enter the High Street, we are pleasantly surprised, the High Street is not too big or too small. People are friendly and know each other. We walk round and we have a meal. We then pray for a place to put up the banner. As we go around a sticker pen and health information is put into our hands by staff of Chiltern Radio. Their car is on the pavement and they are letting people know about their radio station. We go back to the main High Street, people are playing musical instruments and classical music. We place our banner by a walled tree. We pray for people to be touched. Jesus answers our prayer and gives us encouragement. A young man on a visit from Belfast comes and speaks, he is a Christian. His mother had taken him to church as a child. She is a Christian herself, in 1994 he gave his life to the Lord. His wife is a Christian too. He leaves, a lady comes up and asks about the Journey, after answering her question she too leaves. A lady is playing her violin with background music.

Luton Shopping Centre
125

Next a gentlemen comes from Northern Ireland, he is full of excitement about the Christian Revival in Florida America, led by Todd Bentley. Trevor Baker who has been to Florida and is now ministering to people in Dudley England. There have been many healings in both countries. He has been to several churches in the Luton area and has been to the Luton Charismatic Church. We are encouraged by various Christian ladies who come up and say "be encouraged." There are baby starlings being fed in the High Street by their parents and there is a little yellow bird which sings beautifully. Our banner is near Primark Store, as we stand a man comes with his guitar, his singing is as flat as a pancake, the songs are full of despair, he sings them again and again. His friends come along and he ends up chatting. A man who was the worse for wear comes and looks at the banner. He goes away, he sits down on a wall, comes back and has another look and goes on his way. Many people look at the banner, others read it aloud, "Journey of the Christian Faith." A young man comes and takes a photo.

There are people wearing T shirts with pictures of skulls, one man has dark trousers with a mid length coat to match. It looks rather like a cape. A police car goes up and down with a fire engine. The police come out of the car and question a young man with a motor bike. There are posters to stick your chewing gum on. The day like Sunday is hot. We enjoy our afternoon. We decide to put down the banner and go back to the bed and breakfast, we pray that many people were touched. There are all sorts of cultures here, the colours of the clothes are beautiful with all manner of dress, people from Pakistan, Ghanian, other parts of African. Jamaican, English. As in all other cities thee is a wonderful array of culture. We do not have to travel far to the nations, they are here alive and vibrant.

We are reminded of the beginning of the book of Acts. Jesus tells his disciples, "Do not leave Jerusalem but wait for the gift My Father promised, which you have heard Me speak about. For John baptised with water, but in a few days you will be baptised in the Holy Spirit." At the day of Pentecost the Jews gathered from all nations as by this time they are scattered across the world. They thought Peter was drunk. The Holy Spirit descended and it was like fireworks cascading down, there was a sound of a strong wind blowing through, tongues of fire came down, many languages were spoken everywhere. The people were astonished, they asked how they could be saved, Peter tells them by repenting, accepting Jesus as their Saviour, by being baptised in water and being baptised in the Holy Spirit, many people repented of their sins and were baptised that day. This is what revival is about, praying, expecting that the Holy Spirit will come down and many people will be touched. In the Isle of Lewis Scotland in 1949 a man named Duncan Campbell led a Christian revival and people on the farms were falling in the Spirit, young people dancing in the barns came running ito the church. Today in Florida USA, and Dudley England, people are are finding the Lord. A man called Gipsy Lee is telling people about Jesus just as the evangelist Gypsy

126

Smith did many years ago, people are being saved and healed. We must go out, evangelise, Jesus will send the Holy Spirit if we cry out to Him. Jesus said to Nicodemus, "The wind blows where it pleases, you can hear its sound, but you cannot tell where it comes from or where it goes, so it is with everyone born of the Spirit." John 3: 8. In 1901 the Pentecostal movement began in America by the power of the Holy Spirit. Keep praying for this nation for our people. Jesus will answer, we only have to ask and have the boldness to go out and tell people about Him, Jesus will do the rest.

We travelled 67 miles from Oxford to Luton in Bedfordshire.

Tuesday 1 July

Today we travel for Luton to Cambridge. We have been well looked after by Ron and his wife Dorothy. Their garden is one of the longest we have ever seen. We see from the bedroom window next doors garden cat. He goes out of the conservatory to the garden, he looks back as he seems to want to stay in. Ron writes out a guide to exit the area for our next location, then we set off. As we come to a roundabout there is a loud smash. Two vehicles have crashed. The drivers are unhurt, they exchange information. We go on our way. As we go along we notice that the harvest is growing, there is a field of white flowers and poppies seemed to have strayed in. We take a photograph.

Lots of grass is now being cut, there is a sweet smell of hay. A lorry is in front of us and there are bales of hay that loses some of its load and flys into the air. We are on our way to Royston and pass a church. At first there is a poster with the scripture, 'I am the Bread of Life.' There are notices telling you how friendly the Church is and all are one. Right by these notices is a notice which says CCTV camera here, which is quite amusing. We drive alongside a railway line and blue and red coloured trains go past with electricity lines going along overhead. We pass a sign saying Radio Station.

Between Luton and Cambridge

127

There is a lavender field and it's perfume gently comes across the field into the car. We look for a cafe with outside chairs and tables so that we can keep an eye on our car and luggage, we stop at a farm called Bury Lane Farm, the farm shop has everything from farm produce, jams, to ornaments. The cafe is too far away to keep our eye on our car with our luggage. We pray for a cafe with an outside cafe near a car park, our prayers are answered within minutes, we find a place called County Gardens at Royston which has an outside cafe with a car park near by. We have refreshments in the sunshine and watch an adult black bird feeding a baby one, they walk round together, the mother picks up big chunks of food, the baby opened its beak wide and down it goes, it is an amusing sight. We continue on our way to Royston where there are thatched roofs. We arrive into Cambridge passing a football stadium, a golf course and a group of cows on a common. A man pedals across the road with his rickshaw, there are bikes everywhere. We find our bed and breakfast, we register in. A back door is unlocked for us to bring the luggage through. The back door shuts, we have to walk through the front door back to the back door to open it. We try to open the bedroom door, the door won't open, we realise that we have the previous bed and breakfast's keys. We ring Ron to let him know that we have his keys. We get ready to go out.

We walk towards the bus stop, there is a young woman sitting there, we ask her if we are at the right bus stop, she confirms that we are. We sit down and wait. The lady asks about our banner in its case. Colin asks her to guess what it is, she keeps guessing, Colin asks her if she is a Christian, she says "yes." Colin explains about the 'Journey of the Christian Faith'. The bus arrives and we get on. While we are on the bus the young lady tells us that she has been to the Christian event Spring Harvest since the age of 5 and has been this year. We speak about Frenzy at Stornoway, she tells us of another youth event run by the Pioneer Church. She goes to a lively Church of England in Cambridge. Soon it is time to alight from the bus. We say good bye, we have enjoyed meeting our new friend.

We go into the city and walk into the pedestrianised areas and down to the

Market Place which is windy. We find a British Home Stores where we have a meal. We pray for a place to put our banner as it is very windy. We pass a Church called Holy Trinity with a building called Henry Martyn Hall to our left and in front of us is the University Church of which we take a photo. Henry Martyn was a missionary who went out to India, to a plantation in the 1700s, he was ordained in the Church of England, he died young in India.

We place the banner outside Marks & Spencers and wait, the weather is hot. A lady goes past, she smiles and blesses us. She comes back again, she lives in Cambridge, and has been a Christian since a baby. She wonders if Christians need to be bolder in telling others that we are Christians. She went to a posh meeting at college with her daughter where the Principal told people that he was a Christian. She did not seem to think many people would come and chat to us, she was right. No one came. A young lady passes on her bike, she yells, "Yuk, Religious." A man comes along, he plays his guitar. Then two men opposite come to a shop doorway, play their guitars and sing. Sadly the language of the songs is not that nice. We pray that it will stop, thankfully it does. There are an assortment of people passing. A couple go along shouting at each other as if they are in a soap opera. There are problems here as there are in other cities, we pray for these people. At 5 o'clock we decide to leave.

Weslyian Methodist Church Cambridge

We go across the park to look at a Weslyian Methodist Church, we see the minister's name Dr Peter Graves, we know of him as we have heard his name on Premier Christian Radio. The Church has services for students. We take some photos.

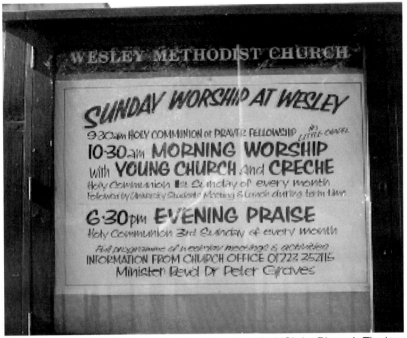

We then travel to the bus stop, the place is called 'Christ Pieces'. The bus stop is the wrong one. We try another, it is still the wrong one as it has been changed. We try again, we go onto the bus, the driver does not know where the road is that we need for our bed and breakfast. We go past our destination, the driver directs us back down the road with another road name. We alight, we walk round, we are getting tired, a cyclist directs us to shops, we feel a presence of angels, we find a car driver and ask directions praying for Jesus to get us home. The driver offers us a lift. We are so grateful. He too has had help in France when he had broken down so he is repaying that kindness. We arrive at the bed and breakfast. Thank you Jesus.

We are reminded of the parable of the Good Samaritan in Luke 10:30, the story Jesus told of the Samaritan and his kindness and love for a wounded man. In Jerusalem was a road called the Bloody Way for obvious reasons. Many people passed this way, there were traders carrying expensive wares like cloth. Along this road on each side were rocks, along these rocks were robbers who were armed with knives, many people were attacked on this route. The Priest and Levites would pass through this road to the temple.

Jesus places the story in this setting. 'A man travels along the road, the thieves see him and come down, they attack and rob him, they take his clothes, he is left for dead. Along comes a Priest, he looks at the man, he looks round and goes to the other side of the road, pretending the man is not there. A little while later, a Levite comes along, a man who does temple duties with the priest, he looks at the man, he then looks round to see if there are robbers watching and passes to the other side of the road, ignoring him. Time passes, a man from Samaria is coming along with his donkey, he takes pity on the man and gives him first aid, he gently lays the man onto his donkey and carries him to an inn. He nurses him all night. He carries on his journey in the morning, leaving money to pay for their expenses and for the man to stay and offers to pay any extra money when he travels through again. A Samaritan was looked upon with suspicion by the Jews and not liked by them'. Jesus said, "If you do it for one of those you do it unto me. If you only help those who help you then what use is that, love your brother, love your neighbour as yourself, bless those who spitefully use you, love your enemies." Jesus has told us to do these things through the Gospels. We have a Good Samaritan Jesus, How about you!!

We travelled 37 miles from Luton to Cambridge.

2 July Friday

Today we travel from the hotel to our next destination Ipswich. The weather this morning is very hot. We travel past fields, there are no animals here, there are more crops and hedges. The greens of the field seem less dark, they are a light green. We pass New Market where there is a horse race course and there is also an Anglican Museum. We pass a football ground, going into the City we see a full Gospel Church and Ashcroft Hall Christian Fellowship. We see two radio stations advertised, one being BBC Radio Suffolk. We book into the bed and breakfast and refresh ourselves, we sort out the computer as it has not been sending out e-mails. We again check the computer and the problem is sorted. The weather is changing, it is cooler, and its feeling damp, very different from yesterday.

We go forth with brollies, it is starting to rain, we find a Christian bookshop on our way, they have a network of fifteen shops in the United Kingdom. We introduce ourselves and take a photo. We then walk towards the High Street, as we enter the streets are wide and well looked after. We go round and pray for a spot, we find one and then go to the local Debenams for lunch. As it is raining we stand outside Lloyds TSB but later we move further up between two pillars at the entrance to an arcade.

Ipswich Christian Bookshop

The 'Journey' team stood in the Market Place opposite the Town Hall and are interviewed & filmed by Christian British media.

Ipswich Town Hall

We have a phone call from Jan Green of Christian British Media asking us for a TV interview on location to which we agree. We pray for the rain to stop which it did although it is still a grey day. A man comes up and speaks then a Welsh lady comes up and speaks of the importance of the Ten Commandments. She is a widow, her husband was a Pastor and used to give out leaflets on the Ten Commandments. The Ten Commandments she tells us lead to Jesus Christ. Her husband died February of this year. She feels that it is important to get the public's attention. She is going to attend the Conference in Aberwysyth with Pastor Jeff Thomas whom we met in Aberwysyth. She is waiting to meet her son.

Chatting to passers by in Ipswich & Chatting to Film Crew

We meet the Pastor of River of Life Church, John McKintosh, who heads up the team working on the streets, speaking and witnessing. He is using part of his time doing this alongside Simon and Robin who are also street evangelists and they are using Birmingham Gospel tracts. Robin started the outreach on his own, Simon and John eventually joined him. They are from different churches, they have been encouraged to do more outreach. While Robin, Simon and John were speaking, Jan and David come to interview us. A lady comes by and heckles us, she points at the banner and shouts, "it is all about death." The Welsh lady responds, "It is all about life, life in Jesus." Everyone is talking, another man, David, tells us that he has been having mental health problems but has been building up his life by studying law by correspondence. He plays chess and belongs to a chess club, he confesses a form of faith that he believes that Jesus takes away our life of sin, that there is forgiveness and salvation, he cannot accept that Jesus is God. We meet quite a few people, some are Christians, some are not. the ones who are not Christians are quite mixed up, more often not having clear Christian teaching in our view.

Jan and David are ordained ministers' of the Christian Church, they have a good afternoon meeting people on the street. The British Media TV aims to bring British Christian Projects to people's attention, it is a project of Green Pastures Christian Trust reaching English people rather than the American TV. Its launching is summer 2008, to present the British Church to the nation through TV and the Internet. We end the afternoon in prayer. We say farewell to everyone. We take down the banner and return to the bed and breakfast.

As we think of the people in the streets, chatting to them, many are non Christians who are not aware of sin. As Christians we know that we do wrong and try to correct it through our faith in Jesus. Non Christians do not know sin and carry on as the 'world' tells them, that it is all right to take other peoples wives and husbands leaving behind a devastated husband or wife and probably children who are left without a parent. A one night's pleasure ending with a child on the way, the mother has the child, the father wants to see his child but often cannot bringing further pain for a night of pleasure. A person having a night of drinking enjoying his evening, he gets into the car, an accident happens, a person dies, another family loses a person, all for a night of pleasure drinking and enjoying oneself without thinking of the consequences. Sin brings devastation, misery and destruction of life for ourselves and those around us, having faith in Jesus helps us to stay on the right path. We are reminded of the story of Simon the Pharisee who invited Jesus into his house as recorded in Luke 7:36. A lady comes into the house with her alabaster jar of perfume. In those days that was like an insurance for her, she would save this perfume for her wedding day, without this perfume she probably could not marry, it was her life savings. She came to Jesus, she was a prostitute. She wept, her tears fall upon His feet, she kissed and dried His feet with her hair. Simon was angry, he did not want the woman around, the woman was a sinner, why should Jesus allow her to touch Him. Simon would have gone and washed himself straight away if the lady had touched him as he would have been tainted. Jesus knew what Simon was thinking and told him a story. He said to Simon, "Two men were in debt, they owed money to a money lender, one owed five hundred denarius, and the other fifty denarius, the money lender told them to forget about their debts. Who was the most grateful?" Simon thought about this, "The one who owed the most I suppose," he answered. "Correct." answered Jesus. Jesus explained to Simon that he did not do his job as a proper host. In those days guests when they entered the house were given water to wash their feet, they were greeted with a kiss and oil was poured upon their head. Simon had done none of these things. The woman had. She was forgiven many sins by Jesus because she tended to Him with love and care. Simon cared little for Jesus, he ignored Him as a guest. the lady made a fuss of Jesus. Jesus again spoke to Simon, the woman had given Him love, yes she had sinned a lot but she was forgiven. Simon had little love for Jesus, he did not see himself as a sinner and despised those who were. Jesus told her that her faith had made her whole. She had demonstrated her faith in Jesus by caring for him, her life had been changed and this was her act of love.

Is it not wonderful that no matter how bad we have been that Jesus forgives us by His mercy even though we do not deserve it. Amen

We travelled 54 miles from Cambridge to Ipswich in Suffolk.

We have an early breakfast and head for Maidstone. We drive past a sign with the words 'Welcome to Essex.' We pass two tin cabins which are cafes. The first one has flags flying. There are trees and fences dividing the fields instead of stone walls or hedges. As we go along, to our right is a river in the distance with barges. We see many pylons and wires across the fields. To our left we pass a farm with horses. The fields start to go a slightly darker green, the sunlight glides across lighting them up. Hills start to emerge with trees upon them with trees in front of us, street lights start to appear in the middle of the road with fences. They are tall and greyest white in colour, then single lights appear on the side grass verges, we drive towards Dartford and the Thames Estuary, the grass has been cut. We go across the Dartford Bridge, the view is awe inspiring. On our right you can see London and the docklands, the Thames Estuary and the London ships, on our left is a great expanse of water road ships. As we drive off the bridge there is a sign welcoming us to Kent. As we continue to drive we pass a Hop Farm on the way to Maidstone a reminder of the days when people went on holiday to the Hop Fields with their families earning an income as well as having fresh air and a holiday in some form. We pass Arlington Baptist Church.

As we were early we find a village and have a break. We leave and we sign in at the next bed and breakfast. We walk to the town and enter Maidstone town, it is very pretty. Maidstone is a Medieval town, there is the Archbishops Palace which was originally built for the Archbishops of Canterbury and is now a Council office. In this town the Battle of Maidstone took place in 1648 between the Roundheads and Cavaliers. In 1647 Parliament did not want the traditional Christmas celebrations and tried to change them, in Canterbury and London there was uproar which went into riots across the country. The rioters were asking for King Charles I to have full power in the country again. The English Parliament's position was becoming perilous with problems in South Wales supporting the Cavaliers, followers of King Charles, and a possible invasion into England from Scotland. A man called General Fairfax was marching to Scotland but he was diverted to Kent. General Fairfax mustered his troops at Hounslow Heath, he marched down to Maidstone, while this was happening the Royalists had picked a leader who was the Earl of Norwich in Maidstone. Another leader came onto the scene who was Colonel Hewson who was leading the Parliamentarian advance guard, between General Fairfax and Colonel Hewson there was a massive battle in Maidstone. The Royalists lost, the Earl of Norwich did not fight in Maidstone, he and his army fled to London where he could not enter as they had shut the gates of London on him. In the end the Earl went to Chelmsford with some of his men as many had by now deserted him. Meanwhile in Kent, Maidstone and the other areas of Kent were gradually taken back by the Parliament forces.

We pray for a place to put up the banner. We go to have a meal, while we are eating there is a Black Labrador guide dog who has the most beautiful eyes. We leave the restaurant and go to the place that we have chosen. The wind is strong, we stand opposite the House of Fraser store with two roads facing us and a straight road in between. There is a bicycle tied up onto a waste bin next to the banner as we put it up. A lady in her fifties comes up, she is from the Roman Catholic Church, she is 'born again' and is full of the Lord while she is talking to us, another lady in her twenties comes to untie her bike, she too is Catholic, we all have a good chat. The older lady leaves. The other lady is so pleased that the Ten Commandments and Jesus are being shown. While we are talking two children come up and give us a leaflet. We ask them what the leaflets are, "Jesus loves you." they answer, "That's what it says here." They go and the lady calls to them. The two children call back, "Are you born again?" They ask her. "Yes." she responds, "of Fire and Water." The children go back to their mother waiting with another child for them. We pray with the lady then she leaves, she is very spirit filled. The leaflets are from "Victory Tracts', London.

Many people looked at the posters. There are lots of young people here. It is a general meeting place for young people and others. People pass through all the time. There are tourists here. It is a windy afternoon, it is hard to keep the banner in place, we use a long umbrella to keep it steady. One man comes, he asks questions and then goes. Soon it is time to finish. We put away the banner and walk back to the bed and breakfast. As we walk back we see a statue to World War II, it has St George standing with the dragon at his feet, he is holding a banner with a cross. His dress looks very Puritan.

When we look at Matthew 4 we see the battle between Jesus and Satan, Jesus fasted for forty days and nights in the desert. Jesus was hungry, the devil came and said to Him, " if you are the Son of God you can make these stones into bread." Jesus told him that man does not just live on bread that keeps him alive physically, but on every Word that comes from the mouth of God that keeps him alive spiritually. The devil tries again, he takes Jesus to Jerusalem, right to the highest top of the synagogue, "Go on, Jesus, if you are the Son of God, throw yourself off, the angels will save you from falling."' Satan here is quoting scripture from Psalm 91:11-12. Jesus answers him back with another scripture, Deut 6:16, "It is written." He answers "Do not put the Lord your God to the test." Jesus is telling the devil, He, Jesus is God. We have to remember that Jesus is in a humans body at this point in time. The devil tries again, he takes Jesus to a mountain, he offers Jesus all the kingdoms and their splendour to the God who created them asking Jesus to worship him. Jesus tells him to go away and He again quotes scripture, "Worship the Lord your God and Him only." The devil defeated leaves, we are told that the angels came and attended to Jesus. Deutronomy 6:13.

In 2 Thessalonians 15 we are told 'so then brothers, stand firm and hold onto the teachings we passed on to you whether by word of mouth or by letter.

Hold firm to your faith, Jesus will keep you on a steady path. He is the bread of life.

We travelled 91 miles from Ipswich to Maidstone in Kent

4 July Thursday

Today we travel from Maidstone to Brighton. We pass factories and fields of cows and horses. The weather is warm, we pass the Railway Mission. There are many seagulls and when we arrive in Brighton we find that the bed and breakfast is not suitable, we try another with the same problem, we pray, at last we find one. We hurriedly change and go into town by bus. There are flowers of many colours which are pretty. We alight from the bus and pass a shop which is plastered in Tarot cards. There seems to be a lot of French people here. A lot of males seem to be wearing earrings mainly blue coloured. We look round and pray for a place to put the banner. At last we find a place, we leave and have a meal, we go back to a place called Churchill Square.

Churchill Square Brighton

We pray again for the right spot, we decide to place the banner by some steps where we feel we would not be in the way of people, there are many young people here. There are groups meeting here to chat with their friends and people going into the HMV Store. There are two cafes nearby for drinks. Two security guards come flying out, they ask us to leave as it is private ground. We ask for clarification, we point out that we are not selling and only here for a few hours, a one off. We were not harming anyone, there was no notice saying that we were on private property. They were rude about the

137

banner and threatened to have us arrested. they say the police are coming but the police are too busy chasing criminals thieving. The security guards at last gave us a letter clarifying the situation.

We leave and go to the beach promenade, we are near Brighton Pier, we meet thousands of people on this hot day. Nearby there is bungy jumping on the beach which attracts many people, there too on our left is a Scottish piper playing Scottish music. People come up and put money into a bag on the ground. Then to our right is a man dressed in silver moving slowly on a stool waving to people, he looks a bit like the tin man in the Wizard of Oz. Another man comes and he does reggae dancing, he is being filmed by his friend, Two young ladies come and watch, one young lady is filmed. The piper laughs at this. A woman who is dressed as a wood nymph in green goes up to the piper and listens. There are many tourists from other countries. There are a lot of young people from abroad. Many look at the poster. A young man says "God loves you" to his mates. A lady looks, many people look and speak about the banner between themselves. A lady comes past, "Praise the Lord" she exclaims, "keep the good work up." A man goes by with his family, "Praise the Lord," he says. Another man comes and takes a photo.

Promenade in Brighton

Two young women tourists come up to us and they speak. They are pleased that the message covers the Protestants and Roman Catholics. It is an interesting afternoon. We finish a 5 o'clock, we have refreshments on the beach. There again are loads of young people here, some at tables others walking by, they are aged from about 13 to 18 years of age, they are going to a disco further up the beach where there is a huge queue. Here in the cafe there is a group of men from the Midlands, three of whom go onto the Carrousel nearby which is playing the Lambeth Walk song as the horses go round. They look as it they are in a comedy as every time they came round they move positions waving to their mates. There is a table of youngsters who are not behaving very well. We have our meal and go. There are many young people now in the queues for the discos, they are being searched by security guards, they hand in their identity cards and then are allowed in. We walk back onto the pavement, a policeman looks down at the youngsters from the bridge. We see a man being taped into newspaper. A girl is wearing a 'Jesus Loves You' belt. We get onto the bus back to the bed and breakfast.

The Lord gives us Psalm 14, 'The fool says in his heart, there is no God, they are corrupt, their deeds are vile, there is no-one who does good. The Lord looks down from Heaven on the sons of men to see if there are any who understand, any who seek God. All have turned aside, they have altogether have become corrupt, there is no-one who does good, not even one. Will evil doers never learn, those who devour my people as men eat bread, and do not call on the Lord. There they are, overwhelmed with dread, for God is present in the company of the righteous. You evil doers frustrate the plans of the poor, but the Lord is their refuge. Oh, that salvation for Israel would come out of Zion! When the Lord restores the fortunes of his people, let Jacob rejoice and Israel be glad.'

John 8:34-36 is very clear about what Jesus said, "I tell you the truth, everyone who sins is a slave to sin. Now a slave has no permanent place in the family but a son belongs to it forever. So if the Son will sets you free, you will be free indeed." There is hope, hope through Jesus. This is the message of Jesus, we have been set free from sin. Let us take the Good News of Jesus into our cities, in our towns, villages where ever we are. Jesus is the Good News, He has set us free now, let us tell others so that they too may have the chains of bondage broken. Amen

We travelled 65 miles from Maidstone to Brighton East Sussex.

5 July Saturday

Today we leave Brighton, we sally forth to Portsmouth. Outside our bed and bedfast while we are preparing to leave, we have a view of flags, one is the Union Jack. We listen to the news. The news today is about women bishops being discussed at the Synod Meeting and President Maugabee, his treatment of people and proclamation as leader. People are packing their bags and leaving, unable to stay in Zimbabwe any longer. We drive out into the countryside, we see a traditional windmill and it looks very cheerful in the countryside. We pass many cows and Arundel Castle. We cross the River Ford and pass Fontwell racecourse and nestling in the hills is Chichester Cathedral. We come into Hampshire and pass the Earnley Baptist Church with a road called the Middlesex Road. Years ago Middlesex was a county although it has gone people still use it on their postcode. The borough of Hounslow is still one of the areas where some people use it as an address with their postcode.

Downs from Brighton to Portsmouth

We pass a cemetery and opposite is a pub called the Gravediggers Pub which has a picture of two men digging with their spades. The sat-nav speaks, we arrive at the bed and breakfast, we are early. As we sit in the car and wait a lady is singing Motown music from one of the houses, she is very good. Soon we are in the bed and breakfast. We go to the bus stop near by, we get onto the bus, we look out of the window, there is a lovely boating pool, the view is beautiful. We go past a small town with an outdoor market, soon we are in the bigger town. We alight off the bus. We walk round and pray for a spot in the centre. We then go for lunch and come back.

We see a plaque telling us that this is the town where Charles Dickens was born. Anyone who has read his books will realise what a good writer he was. One of his books, 'A Tale Of Two Cities,' is based on a man sacrificing his life for his friend, the story is based in the time of the French Revolution. Sydney Carton, a character in the story, has fallen in love with a young lady called Lucy, who falls in love with someone else, and whom she marries. Her husband Charles Darnay is French and is tricked in going back to France where he is put into prison to be executed. Sydney who is similar in looks goes over to France and swaps places with Charles Darnay, he is guillotined in place of his friend. The story is based on Jesus dying on the Cross, sacrificing his life so that we might live, Sydney gave up his life for love of his friend so that she could have her husband back alive, he could have married her himself if her husband had died, he chose not to do this. Jesus gave his life up because He too loves us so that we might live and have eternal life. He took our sins upon Himself so that we can be forgiven, if only we would turn to Him. Charles Dickens was a man who wrote about his faith, he was a reformer, he wrote articles on the slave trade and injustice of how people were treated. He lived at the time of George Muller who opened the Muller Homes for street children. George Muller was a man who lived by faith and waited for the Lord to provide food and funds for each day. George came from Germany realising that God wanted him to help these children in England. Charles Dickens visited him in Bristol and wrote an article about his work. Charles Dickens books are full of good and evil, he shows through his stories that evil does not pay. He, himself, saw groups of children taught by adults to thieve, Oliver Twist is an example of this. There are many Fagins gangs around today. Part of Oliver's Twist's walk to London starts at Isleworth in the London Borough of Hounslow. The Inn where Charles Dickens stayed is still there today, it was a coaching inn in those days, its name still is The Coach and Horses. Charles took a walk past the houses and roads which are in the novel Oliver Twist, little has changed in this part of Isleworth today.

Shopping Centre Portsmouth

We pray for somewhere to put the banner, there is a spot near a fountain with seats. There are many young people gathered here, it is their meeting place. They are aged from 13 years to 15 years of age. One has a child, another is pregnant. They use basic street language. They hug and kiss each other. They talk about getting pregnant as normal, they talk about gayness, slags and perverts. If a boy upsets them, they call them perverts. There is no moral code, there is nothing. It is like a dandelion clock being blown by the wind landing anywhere. It can do anything. These young mums are like a growing child going into adulthood, trying to look after a baby who is trying to toddle and is trying to grow into a child, each one at different stages of childhood, one not understanding the other as they go through their growing stages. It is tragic that these young people seem to have no-one to guide them, no-one to tell them right from wrong. An older woman who is a single mum goes past with a baby, she is telling a male friend about boy friends who are asking her out. These people need Jesus, they need Christians to tell them that God loves them so much that He sent his Only Son to die for them. They do not always have parents or grandparents or relatives to tell them this message.

Nearby there is 'Shelter', the homeless charity, telling people about homelessness . One man comes up and asks us what we are carrying. To our left in the square representatives of the Labour Party were celebrating sixty years since the conception of the National Health Service. We have lived in a country where for years we have had a good health service, whereas before people had to pay a GP to come out for a visit to their home. Many women after the war were widowed and had large families they had to pay for each child, there was no benefits or help as there is today, this was in a era before vaccinations could protect us from polio, tuberculosis, etc. We are so fortunate to live in a day and age to have treatment on the National health system, to be able to go to the doctor when we want and for our GP's to come out at night. We take so much for granted, we are very privileged to live in a society to have this treatment.

Sea Front at Portsmouth

We put the banner up, two people pass and read the message out loud. No-one comes near. We finish at 5 o'clock and go. We go back to the bed and breakfast, we put our things into the house and walk to the huge boating pool, there are hugh white boats with the shape of Swans, we walk along the promenade. There is a pier with amusements, a shop which is shutting and a reception area. We keep walking, we can see the car ferry to the Isle of Wight.

There are two old ships in the waters from the war. We met a lady who tells us about Henry VIII's castle, we go up to have a look, there is a pathway which goes up and there is a stone wall to our right. There is a cannon facing the water, the castle is open to the public. It does seem incredible that here Henry VIII visited and through him the Church divided. At the moment the Anglican Synod is meeting, it again is split with one group of bishops meeting a Lambeth Palace and another group of Bishops meeting in Israel. The division came with Henry's stance against the Pope. It was also felt that women were not suitable candidates for the throne. Catherine was a dedicated Catholic and her daughter was Mary Tudor who was to inherit the throne before Elizabeth I, Henry's daughter by Ann Boleyn. Across the water, as we look centuries later, on the Isle of Wight another King, King Charles I, was held prisoner at Carisbrook Castle. Charles I was later executed. The Puritan movement had begun and was again like the Protestant movement that was to affect the whole country in its Christian faith and have a Republic for the first time in England's history.

142

Looking out to the Solent with the Isle of wight in the distance

Today, again, the Protestant Church of England is changing, it is being moulded, reformed and shaped by various hands. It is like the Church is going through an old fashioned mangle being pressed with certain things gone, the Church of England is going through another Reformation. We walk back, we go past the pier, there are old fashioned shops being pulled down and rebuilt. Sometimes the Church has to be torn down and rebuilt on the Gospel rather than man's religion, as God reforms it and changes it to the way He wants. We walk back to the bed and breakfast.

Today we think of Ninevah. the city grew wicked, God asked Jonah to go and preach to them. He did not want to go. Why should he? he asked, the people were bad, let them stew. He did not want to mix with them. Jonah ran off onto a ship heading for Joppa, God created a storm, the sailors realise that Jonah was the cause. He was thrown overboard and a whale swallowed him up. He stayed in the whale until the Lord made the whale spit him out. Jonah reached Ninevah in the end and gave them God's message, we are told that a visit to Ninevah took three days. The people were given forty days to repent. They thought about this, and did repent, they said that they were sorry for what they had done. We need to give the message, it does not matter if we do not get on with the person or that their life style does not suit us. They have the right to hear the Good News just as we have. Why should they be saved; because we were once all sinners. Jesus says if we only love those who love us then it is useless. We must embrace everyone. Jesus saved you, He saved me. He could have left us to do what we like and not died on the Cross for us, He died for you, He died for me, He died for everyone because He loves us.

"Come follow me" said Jesus, not just some but everyone, all of you are precious to Him."

We travelled 51 miles from Brighton to Portsmouth in Hampshire.

Today we leave Portsmouth for Bournemouth, the day is wet, the rain is teeming down. We arrive in Bournemouth and we have a break in our car on the sea front by the surfing club. The car park is full of surfers and their cars. We can see people bobbing up and down in the sea. we pray to Jesus for calm weather. We remember the story of Jesus in the boat, and the disciples woke Him up as they were afraid. Jesus awoke and calmed the sea, the disciples realise that Jesus is God. Our prayers are answered, the wind and rain die down and we go to the bed and breakfast. We take our banner and set forth, we walk along the sea-front and towards the Terrace Gardens. The carousel is going round as we pass. We move determinedly on amidst the small shops, we pass a bandstand on our right and people are playing crazy golf on our left. The sun is now shining as we start to come out of the gardens, to our right there is an air balloon which is out of action because of the high winds. We then pass a cafe and walk up the steps of the Terrace Gardens across the road into the town square praying as we go. In front of us is a crowd of people are following a band playing music moving towards the bandstand. The musicians have stag heads on, they look like the devil. They have a black banner, it feels like the pits of Hell. They end up at the bandstand, the stag heads are removed, they carry on playing. They are playing in front of us on the left. On the right of us are people dressed in white feathers and robes, they seem to be dressed as angels. We pass through to the town, praying for the right place. We pray again for a spot for the banner, we find one and we put the banner up and stay there. A lady comes and takes two leaflets, later a Rastafarian comes, we chat. He has a lot of Bible knowledge from the Book of Revelation and the end times. He suddenly points to where the musicians are playing. "Look," he said, "the Mark of the Beast." People turn and looks. He thinks that the world will last about another fifty years, the musicians play Abba and other tunes. The Rastafarian then bids farewell and leaves.

Bournemouth Square

The band finishes with God Save The Queen, people dance, a band dressed as Beefeaters wait to play. Their red sharply contrasts with the black. It was like the blood of Christ flowing Crimson. His blood shed for our dark sins. The other band put back on their stag heads, the black banner goes forth into the darkness. It was like the devil was leading people into Hell with his demons. People clapped and cheered, they wave the band good-bye. One day the Lord said it will be the other way round. Jesus Himself will come again and judge the living and the dead, the devil and his cohorts, the prince of this World will be cast out forever into hell. The Beefeaters come on and play, red against the whiteness of the other band.

We decide to move, the banner seems to be in a dark place being eclipsed by a shadow. We look for another place. We go over and look across the way. There is a young lady selling the Big Issue. We give her some money for her magazine. She breaks down and cries. We chat to her and we ask if she has faith. "What has God done for me," she asked. She has been reading the Bible asking for help and does not seem to find it. We pray in Jesus Name to help her. She is afraid that she might be picked up by men in the street. We have come across this before, some women find themselves on the street. The government has said that they are not vulnerable unless they have children, sadly pimps come along, they try to pick them up for prostitution and sometimes men sleeping rough want them as well. Em's grandmother was a drinker and Em's mother died from cancer. Em and her father moved to another area, he then also dies from an illness. She is on her own with no family and homeless. She was on the Council list but without a base that night, she does not have enough money. We arrange to meet her later.

We leave the Terrace Square, walk back to the Terrace Gardens and put up the banner near where the crazy golf is. A man comes up with his female companion, he is from London and tells us not to help Em as he has seen plenty of women like her in London, he has seen us talking to her. He tells us there is a great Church in Bournemouth, to put down our banner and enjoy our holiday. We decide not to. We pray and ask the Lord to let us know what He wants. The Lord reminds us of the story of the Good Samaritan and we decide to meet Em as arranged. Three young Christians come to speak to us, they are from Guildford, we chat to them, it is such a thrill to meet them. Praise the Lord for these young believers. We pray that they will lead their friends to the Lord. Soon it is time to put the banner away. We do this, we sit down and wait for Em, she arrives and we chat, soon we are looking for a bed and breakfast for her so that she is safe for the night. We pass some classic cars, there are people filming them. At last "Praise the Lord," we find a place for her. We see her into reception, after signing in we say good-bye and leave. We feel such a feeling of peace. Hopefully one day Em will find Jesus. As we walk home the dark clouds send us heavy rain, we walk along the pier, the sand, wind and rain blow in, people sit in their beach huts cosy, others in cafes sipping tea. We would like a paddle in the sea but resist the urge. We arrive at the bed and breakfast looking as if we have swam in the sea rather than walking past it.

Thinking about Em and her situation we are reminded of Matthew 5:27 we are warned about adultery, it is the seventh of the Ten Commandments. Jesus has strong words about this. He tells us that anyone who looks at a woman lustfully has already committed adultery with her in his heart. He tells us if our right eye or our right hand causes us to sin, throw your eye away and cut your hand off, for He warns it is better to lose one part of your body than for your whole body to go to hell. That is how serious sin is. We could have believed that man from London and not help Em, taken down our banner and enjoy that afternoon and go to worship in the Church. The parable of the Good Samaritan in Luke 10 :25, the priest and Levite, two religious men walk by, they have done their duties in the temple but they do not help the man in the road thinking that he may have been put there as a decoy so that when they went to help they would be robbed. The Samaritan cast these thoughts aside and helped the man. If we had followed that man's advice instead of God's, Em would never have known the love of Jesus, we could have been like the priest and the Levite walking by, doing our worship in the local church, keeping the message of the Gospel within the church walls. How Satan would have loved that, the Good News of Christ kept away from his people.

We travelled 52 miles from Portsmouth to Bournemouth.

7 July Monday

Today we leave Bournemouth for Exmouth, we travel towards Devon, we pass a marina with geese upon it. Further on there is a deer, the first one we have seen on the Journey, lying in a field. The fields here are separated by hedges with sheep and cows. We are reminded of Scotland and the sheep with the stone walls dividing the land instead of hedges. We see the sea bathed in sunlight looking crystal clear, the hills have dark trees upon them with sheep here and there. The fields are varied in colours of greens, tans, limes, light brown, the sun lighting up the colours like a torch lightly being waved across. There is rye grass. White and yellow flowers dot the verges splashing them with colour. We go through Chidioch and Charmouth in Dorset. We stop at a motel, the sky is black with rain. We decide to eat outside under a flimsy shade to keep an eye on the car. We order a meal, while we wait the rain descends, it gets heavier and heavier. People going into the cafe look at us amazed as we eat our meal. We have a huge umbrella as the weight of the shade begins to chuck down the water. We managed to eat most of our meal but eventually we have to go inside as we are getting wet. Soon we leave the cafe and continue our journey.

Arriving at Exmouth

We arrive in east Devon. We book into a quiet place, we meet the B&B proprietors Wendy, and her husband who has been a musician. They used to live in Richmond Surrey. They have been on an Alpha course and have Christian friends encouraging them in their faith by inviting them to Christian events. After booking in we drive to the town. We walk round the town and sea front praying. We go to get a drink and continue to look for a place for the banner. One part of the town did not seem appropriate nor did the sea front.

Exmouth Centre and Sea Front

There is a primary school here. We pray again and Jesus leads us to a square with seats in another part of the town. We put up a banner, people are coming up and down. We are opposite a small Sainsburys. We pray for the wind and rain to stop, Jesus answers our prayer. A lady passes and says, "God bless." Another Christian lady passes, she tells us she has been a Christian all her life, she has moved from Cornwall at twenty two years of age. When she leaves, a Muslim man comes up to speak, he is a student, he is from Dubai, he is in England studying languages, he is with a host family but the man of the house does not believe in God but Darwin, he is a very nice man and cannot understand why we as a nation do not want God. He said ninety percent of people are not interested, people do not follow God at home and is not taught in schools. In Dubai faith is taught in the home and schools. He said that a man came with a violin and played, people danced and put money into a hat, but when it comes to God no-one wants to know. He then leaves, another man comes along to chat, he is in his late thirties, he is a professor and asks many questions about the faith. He is not a believer, "what difference does it make to our lives," he asks. "How can it affect your life." He asks about redemption. We explain that Jesus is Lord of our lives, about God's KIngdom, His plans are not our own. "Is God Jesus." He asks and we reply, yes. He asks about young people, he asks many general questions. We have a good discussion. "Thanks very much," he says and leaves.

This gentleman had asked about murder and war, sometimes there are just wars, for instance World War II . We need the mind of Christ. The more we are in Christ the more we will know if it is a just war. People pass by saying "God loves you." One lady passes saying, "It is a load of old rubbish," but at least we are getting reactions. A young female and male student come up. They have a few giggles about adultery and covertness. One jokes that he hoped that he would fail his religious exam and they go. A young woman with her male friend said, "God loves you, through Jesus Christ." It was lovely to hear. We have a good afternoon, at 5 o'clock we fold up our banner and leave. Thankful that the rain had held off.

When we think of the Ten Commandments, especially number 7 that you shall not commit adultery, we can think of the lady who was caught in adultery, John 8:1-11,. In the Bible story she was caught in the act and dragged by the Scribes and Pharisees to Jesus. They take stones to kill her for what she has done. They challenge Jesus by saying that the lady should be stoned, Jesus writes in the ground then He looks up from the ground and answers them. "Let him who is without sin cast the first stone," Jesus continues writing in the ground, men look at each other with the stones in their hands, they drop them and leave, silently one by one. Soon the woman and Jesus are left on their own. They look at each other. "Where are your accusers?" He asks, "They have gone," she answers, Jesus tells her to go and sin no more. If we can reach the person in the street just as Jesus did, the drug addict, the homeless person, the drinker, the broken hearted, the prostitute, they can tell their friends about Jesus, many lives could be changed. Jesus spoke to the woman at the well. One word, one chat, many lives were changed that day. The Holy Spirit can give you the words. A persons life could be changed and many others. "Go and tell every one and make disciples of them, go out on the highways and bye ways, the streets, the places where Jesus went, you too will be glad that you went and Jesus will be too.

We travelled 85 miles from Bournemouth to Exmouth in Devon.

Today we leave Exmouth and travel to Barnstable, North Devon. We pass the fields and hedge groves. We find our bed and breakfast, we are early so we go to the local Sainsburys for refreshment. We go back to the bed and breakfast, it is raining. A painter is working on the bed and breakfast, he moves for us to drive through. We sign into the bed and breakfast and head off for the town, catching a bus, the rain is abating.

Barnstaple Centre

We have been praying for it to stop. We alight off the bus and go to a cafe called Chatterbox for lunch, afterwards we leave the cafe and go forth. The town is busy, there is an indoor market place. The street itself is pedestrianised. We decide to put the banner up under the town clock.

This seems to be an area for dogs and puppies, there is a seat near us where people are sitting. The police are walking up and down, according to the local news, mums walking along with their buggies are being robbed. Two ladies pass us with expandable leads for their two dogs. One dog runs ahead, the dog is pulled back, a man on the seat loses his patience and calls her a name, he is aged about seventy years of age but he is acting like a badly behaved young person. How can any of us expect young people to behave if we act badly ourselves. We must be an example to young people in how to behave because they are watching and copying us.

The afternoon is interesting. A Christian lady comes up from the local Baptist Church. Her Church does work with children coming into church. They have a new Pastor. She realises that there must be more outreach outside the Church. She is very encouraged and said that it was nice to see us. Another lady comes up and says, "God bless you." Another person, a male, walks by and says "God loves you." A young woman walks by with a male friend to a shop across the road and says to him, "God loves through Jesus Christ." Another man reads loudly, "Journey of the Christian Faith." A male Christian comes up and speaks to us, he has grown up in the Brethren Church. He has an uncle who was in the closed Brethren Church. There are two Brethren Churches in Barnstable but they are small in number now. He, himself goes to the Salvation Army as it is nearer for him to get to. He has meals at the Salvation Army and the couple who run the Salvation Army are a Godly couple. Another man comes up, he has worked in London Heathrow Airport and Shepherds Bush. He is widowed, his late wife was a Christian, and he is unable to find a church here. A lady sitting nearby speaks to us too. She asks about the poster, she comes from the Orkneys, she too is widowed and hopes that she will see her husband again and her two dogs who have died otherwise she will not bother going to Heaven. She explains that in the Orkneys, when she dies, her married name will be taken away and her maiden name will be placed onto the grave as they do not want other names in the Orkneys when people are buried there.

The afternoon passes pleasantly, we do find though that the younger people make adverse rude comments towards our banner. We end our afternoon and put down the banner, the weather has been wet, but the Lord honoured our prayer stopping the rain. A little boy laughs at our rainwear. We go to the bus stop. There are shelters for each bus, there is food on the ground, a seagull swoops down, grabs the food and goes. We arrive back at the bed and breakfast, from our window we have a lovely view of the hillsides and the lights are switched on in the houses, they look like coloured beads of a ladies necklace, nestling in the hills.

When we think of outreach in our churches we tend to think of people coming into our churches. How do we get them in? Do we have a modern service, what sort of music? The problem is some people whatever the church provides are not going to come because they are afraid that they will not fit in. Some people are not keen on traditional services. Some who have never seen Church worship will wonder what on earth is going on. Some people will have illnesses where they may not be able to cope with long services. Everyone is different, some have never been to church. Others have had bad experiences. In Brentford, near where we live, there is a Pioneer Church which meets in a swimming baths. We went to a service where men were dancing with banners, the swimmers walked passed looking down through the windows, it was a great witness to them. We were also invited by the Church to a garden party, we chatted to a lady who had just joined, she asked about our Church, we explained that the Church had a cafe where she could have refreshments. "Oh I can't go into a church building." she exclaimed. "Well," we answered "you are not going into a main church just the cafe." "I can't." she answered, "I am afraid, I come here because I do not have to go into a church building." Cafes in churches are a good idea but this lady is not unusual. There are people out there who are adamant that they are not going into a church building. This is a group of people the church needs to address because they are never going to enter your building.

Jesus, Himself realised this. He had to walk and talk, tell stories. He could never stay in the Synagogue and wait for the people to come and hear the Good News of His Father. He would have waited for ever. He went off, picked and taught His disciples how to spread the Good News for others to follow later. If he had not done this there would be no Good News or the Christian Church now. He gave up His job as a carpenter and lived by faith. Jesus came for the lost, He is the shepherd of the sheep, Luke 15. Jesus had got into trouble mixing with the sinners. He rebuked the Pharisees and gave the parable of the Prodigal Son. He tells us a story of a farmer who has two grown up sons, they had an inheritance each, the younger one wanted his money straight away. The father was not happy about this but allowed his son to have his share. The son leaves the farm, he soon spends all his money on wild living as his money is spent, there is a severe famine in the land, he has no money and he is hungry. He gets a job feeding pigs, he is so hungry he wants to eat the pigs food, no one wants to give him food. He thinks about his life and realises that even his dad's staff have food in their stomachs "I am so hungry" he thought, "I am going back home to dad and hope that he will accept me." The son goes back to his dad, his dad sees him from the fields and runs to his son and hugs him." He is so pleased to see him. His son is humbled and sorry for what he has done. His father arranges a party for him. So it is with God our Father, He loves us so much that we are forgiven, He waits longing for us to turn Him.

View of Barnstaple from our bedroom window

Jesus then and as now goes amongst us, knocking on the door of our hearts. Have you told someone today about Jesus and have they received Him. Has He knocked on your door, have you answered. Every time someone receives Him the angels are rejoicing in Heaven over every sinner who repents. Amen.

We travelled 58 miles from Exmouth to Barnstaple.

Today we travel form Barnstable to Plymouth Hoe. We say good bye to the bed and breakfast and to two male cyclists who are travelling from Land's End to John O'Groats, they are cycling a 100 miles a day for charity. The rain is pouring down. We drive off. We pass two fields of sheep, in the second field the sheep are black headed. We drive into a fog, we can see nothing of the countryside. We drive on and the fog clears. We come to a place called Merry Wavy, there is a Wesleyian Chapel called the Mary Tavey Wesleyian Chapel, 1835. We pass a statue of Captain Grenville a seaman from Elizabeth's I Reign. We drive through Dartmoor, on route there is a plaque to the Pilgrim Fathers (Puritans) who so long ago sailed to America from Plymouth in the Elizabethan era on September 6 in 1620 as they were not allowed to worship or meet together in England. William Penn was another such man, a Quaker who went to America to whom Pennsylvania owes its name and the setting of the American Constitution was influenced by William Penn who himself had set up a constitution in Pennsylvania. Philadelphia too was named by William Penn meaning brotherly love for freedom of religion. It is amazing to think of this today. Seeing America, a country in her own right, starting with a group of Englishmen who could not live their way of Christianity and who sailed with their families to practise their Christianity and worship in their own way and formed America into what she is today.

Plymouth Centre

As we come into Plymouth there is a large statue of a silver dove, holding the olive branch, a reminder of the dove going from the Ark of Noah and coming back with the olive branch in her beak showing that there was dry land. Noah realised that the floods were going down. Today when friendships go wrong we put forth the 'olive branch' hoping to put friendship back into that relationship. The Pilgrim Fathers must have felt like that leaving an old land for a new one not knowing what they would find, they set forth putting their faith in a new land. Just as Noah who trusted God travelled in the Ark not knowing where he and his family would end up. A land changed from the one they knew, they saw the land as the dove did with an olive branch, there was hope and new life. Noah came out of the Ark and was given a vine. He became a vinedresser tending his grapes. The dove comes to the Ark with the 'olive branch'. The Holy Spirit comes to us with His Olive Branch, we only have to accept Him. In the Bible the Holy Spirit is represented as a dove when Jesus is baptised by John the Baptist. The Pilgrim Fathers became God's Ambassadors giving America her basis of faith. "I am the vine, you are the branches says Jesus, God the vinedresser, chopping, shaping His vines into the ones he wants.

We pass a pub called Pennycomequick and a tribute to the Armada, we know that Francis Drake was playing bowls in Plymouth when the Spanish Armada came to invade England in 1588, the weather was bad, there were strong winds and the Spanish lost the battle on the sea with the English. We find our bed and breakfast and then set off to Plymouth Town. The streets are busy, we pop into the local Woolworths for a meal.

'Upper Room' Christian Bookshop Plymouth

Through the back door of Woolworths we spot a Christian Bookshop across the road. We have our meal and go to see them. The Christian bookshop is called 'Upper Room' within the Christian Literature Centre. This Centre is run by a delightful couple named Anne and David. Anne's aunt and uncle started the bookshop, their names were Mary and Dick Leonard, after the death of Dick, Mary and her two sisters ran the shop, Anne has now taken over the helm with her husband David. The premises have changed form the original ones. We have our photo taken and go on our way. Anne and David have told us of the Open Air Mission people who are spending a week in the High Street. We go along to find them praying as we went for a place for our banner. We pass a Salvationist selling the War Cry.

We find the Open Air MIssion people, they are evangelising in the High Street. People are listening with interest, a young couple are very attentive listening as the preacher explains that Jesus is the Love of your life. We speak to John, one of the evangelists. He gives us information about the Open Air mission. We say good-bye and go to see the Salvationist who is selling the War Cry. We find him and chat, his name is Robert of the Plymouth Salvation Army. Robert is on fire for the Lord and a lovely man to talk to. We were thrilled to see the War Cry as it is popular with the folk at the drop in centre we run in the Hounslow Salvation Army Church. If you see the War Cry in your High Street do buy it, it suits the people of today and is relevant to everyday life and Jesus. It is easy for people to read, especially those who have learning difficulties and have problems reading. We call our drop in Centre the 'Olive Branch' because the Lord spoke of the dove with the Olive Branch to tell these people of His Love for them.

Open Air Mission' visiting Plymouth Centre

Chatting and praying with local Salvationist in Plymouth Centre

The Salvation Army was started by a man called William Booth in 1865. William was a Methodist minister but later went into a movement called the Methodist New Connection where he met his wife Catherine Mumford. He again became a minister in 1852 and eventually married Catherine. They went out to the poor, the lonely, and the prisoners preaching to them the Good News of Jesus at the Christian Mission in the east end of London which later became the Salvation Army based on the army. The Salvation Army members were often in trouble with the government and often found themselves in prison or they were given a fine for being a nuisance. Today the Salvation Army is well known for the work it does. We have our photo taken with Robert and leave. We go into a shop recess as the rain is coming down and the wind is strong. The rain stops, people pass. One man asks why did God rain on him, making him wet. We respond, so are we. We do not get much feedback but the message was put across. The Centre was quite wide, there are shops on either side. The day is damp. We finish at 5 o'clock and leave.

Jesus, in John 15, talks about the vine and His Father the Gardener, pruning, cutting off bad fruit making it more fruitful. "Remain in me and I will remain in you ." He says. "You will bear much fruit. If anyone does not bear much fruit, he is like a branch that is thrown away and withers. You did not chose Me but I chose you and appoint you to go and bear fruit, fruit that will last. Then the Father will give you whatever you ask in my name. This is my command "Love one another."

We must go out and preach the Word, like the sower sowing seed we have been given the Word, we must go and tell people about Jesus, just as Anne, David, John and the team, Robert selling the War Cry, everyone telling the Gospel in the way Jesus has given them, we all have a calling to give the Gospel. Jesus has come into our lives, sometimes others have told us about Him and so we have fruit to give, fruit that will last, tell everyone about Him. We are the fruit let others eat of that fruit so that many will come to know Him. Amen.

We travelled 67 miles from Barnstaple to Plymouth in Devon.

10 July Friday

We say good-bye to Plymouth and travel to Penzance. The day is bright and sunny, we pass a Roman Catholic Cathedral and a place called Pilgrim Mews. We pass a Victorian statue of a man in a top hat, the verges on either side of us are beautifully manicured. On our right are fields and parks.

We pass a plague on a building on our left with the words 'Ply Corporation Tramways 1923'. We pass a building with two coloured bricks, they seem to be white and red. On the way to Tamar Bridge there is a huge traffic jam which is slow. There has been an accident. One car is on our left on the verge and has the roof sliced off and another car is in the middle of the road on the grass, its window smashed, the bonnet is dented. The police and fireman are standing by, we drive on, the road is now clear, we come to the Tamar bridge, there is an inscription to Isambard Kingdom Brunel 1859. We pass over water and we see the sign 'Welcome to Cornwall.' Tamar is a lady mentioned in the

Bible, she was the daughter of King David, David had many wives and this for Tamar had tragic consequences. A half brother called Amon fell for her. We are told that she was very beautiful, her full brother was called Absalom. David had a nephew called Janadab, Janadab advised Amon to feign illness and get his father David to send Tamar to attend him. Tamar was sent for, she was raped by Amon. Tamar's life was ruined and she would never be able to marry. Amon, after he had done this deed, hated Tamar, although she had pleaded with him not to do the deed, he locked her out of his room. Tamar wore a virgins robe which she had to change and she went to live with her brother Absalom. David was angry with his son's behaviour, Absalom was to kill Amon two years later. King David was again forced to flee from Absalom as he wanted King David's throne, as King David had fled from King Saul years before. This story is recorded in 2 Samuel:13, Absalom also had a daughter named Tamar.

Travelling to Penzance

We pass an area called Catch French, we are on the A38 to Liskeard. We see the armies of solar windmills and go into Pennith, Logan's Law and Hayle. We are driving into Penzance, we have a view of hills, houses and of water although it is misty with the sun shining over. We pray for the weather, we see the sign, 'Welcome to Penzance,' we have arrived. We drive to the bed and breakfast, then we set off for the high street.

We pray to the Lord for a spot, the main street is windy so we go into another street. We find a shop doorway to protect us from the wind. There is a cafe nearby where we have lunch. We sit outside and we notice a pagan shop called the 'Healing Star', it is full of fairies and earth figures. A woman goes in, she is dressed in green top and trousers, she looks like a mother earth. Two doors away was another shop, the 'Silver Witch' that is a jewellery shop selling silver jewels. This is near to where we are seated in a small market place selling second hand goods. There is an old film amongst the videos advertising idle hands make devils work, there is a book with a picture of the devil playing a pipe on four legs in green. The book is inviting us into his world. There seems to be people here who have mental health problems as they chat to each other. In the ladies toilets there is a hole in the wall for syringes from drug addicts. We finish our meal and stand in the empty shop doorway with the banner as the wind is too strong. There are workmen in the shop who come outside to have a look. The street is busy, people are looking. A man comes up, he has dyslexia, we read out the poster to him, he thanks us and goes.

Penzance Shopping Centre

A lady comes along, she asks us about 'Alpha' as she wants to go on the course. We advise her to contact Holy Trinity Brompton who could send her details of a church in the area. She wants to help people in drop in centres but we tell her initially having a personal faith is more important as good works cannot save us. She leaves and a Messianic Jew comes up and shows us his Jewish Bible. Another Christian chats to us, he is from the local Baptist Church. Along comes a curate's wife who comes from Hayle who has been working with her husband in the Church. She is a mixture of Methodist, Pentecostal and Church of England. A lady walks up to us, she is a member of Churches Together Penzance, they are waiting to meet us in another part of town,. Her husband David too, is waiting for us. We fold up our banner and go to meet them.

We meet the team and have wonderful conversations with them all and we have photos taken. Behind us is a statue of Humphrey Davy inventor of the safety lamp in the mines. Opposite us is Market Jew Street where also there is an inn called the Star Inn which we are looking at, beside the inn is a small side road, where there was once a Synagogue where the Jews went to meet. The Methodist movement has been strong in Cornwall, perhaps more so than Presbyterianism in Scotland and Wales. As we look at the Star Inn we can see a balcony where it is said that John Wesley preached from. He visited Cornwall many times, he had many tomatoes and things thrown at him.

There is a man nearby who has a drink problem, he very kindly moves for us so we can take the photos. David chats with him. The local Christians we are meeting have a strong feeling to go out in the streets and tell people about Jesus, we leave the team feeling greatly encouraged, we go back to the bed and breakfast.

When we think about King David's family and the terrible evil of Amon and Absalom we can cast our minds back to the book of Genesis, with the first murder of a brother. Abel killed by his brother Cain who are the sons of Adam and Eve. The devil entered Amon with lust for Tamar, he so much wanted her but his fantasy was more interesting that reality, Tamar pleaded with him not to do it but he would not listen, he ruined her life and his own as he realised when he had done the deed. It was not what he thought. Eve ate the apple, the devil told her it was good to ignore God, after all why should she not eat of the fruit, it looked so good, she did with dire consequences, her family life was ruined, Abel her son got jealous of his brother Cain. Abel looked after his flocks, he loved them, he was the first farmer, his brother was a man of the soil. In those days animals were not eaten but were sacrificed to God, the best of the flock would be given to God as a gift at the altar. The first animal died to give clothing to Adam and Eve who when eating the apple realised that they were naked, their innocence had gone. Cain was proud of what he grew and did not give the glory to God and grudgingly gave him his produce on the altar. God knew this, He was pleased with Abel who always gave God the credit for the animals. One day Abel got jealous of his brother and killed him. He pretended to know nothing about it until God challenged him, for it is said that the blood of Abel cried out for vengeance. Abel was punished and had to roam the earth. David's son Absalom killed his half brother Amon with fatal results. He wanted more power and tried to take his father's throne. Absalom died on a tree, scripture says cursed is a man who dies on a tree. Jesus Himself dies on a cross made from the wood of a tree, Judas hangs himself on one after betraying Jesus realising the consequences of what he has done, an innocent man crucified for money gained in Judas pocket.

Jesus spoke to the people about the Father of Lies the devil, telling them them about Cain and Abel. Jesus is the Life and the Truth and the Way. He tells us that those of us who belong to Him, Jesus calls Satan the Murderer from the beginning. Jesus tells us that everyone who sins is a slave to sin. "If you hold to my teaching, you are really my disciples, then you will know the Truth and the Truth will set you free."

When we go out and proclaim God's Word, we as believers must tell people about the words of Jesus that He is the Life, the Truth and and the Way, there is a needy world out there that is looking for answers that only Jesus can give to take them from a life of sin to the devil to a life Freedom in Christ. Amen. Scripture John 8 Verses 31-47.

We travelled 78 miles from Plymouth to Penzance in Cornwall.

Return to London

Friday 11 July

We rise up at 1 o'clock to travel to London. We are on the road at 2 o'clock in the morning, we notice people walking round to the beach past the bed and breakfast. Some one has put grease on our front car window, it is hard to take off. It gets worse if we use water. We wipe it off as best as we can. We start to drive. People are walking around, chatting, shopping as if it is daytime. We leave the town behind and head towards Hayden. We go along the roads past Hayden. The window's view is getting worse. We realise that we have some washing up liquid, the Lord draws our attention to this. We come to a lay-by and in the darkness squirt on some liquid which clears the window. "Praise the Lord." We give a silent thanks and drive on. Sometimes we drive through pitch darkness. We can see houses dotted in the hills, their lights twinkling across. The sky is a dark pink in velvet blue. Soon the dawn is breaking, the sun comes through very brightly shining in the sky. We find a roadside cafe which is open and have a break. We drive on passing fields of cows and horses, sheep. A plane passes by, we are back in London.

We arrive home at 8am, at 1pm there is a phone call from Marcus of Premier Christian Radio, he gives us a telephone interview. Later in the afternoon we hear the Travel programme talking about the Journey of the Christian faith, we are on the news telling people that we will be in London tomorrow. We then go to our local train station to get our tickets for Oxford Street. We are feeling very tired. We prepare for the next day and go to bed early.

We travelled 307 miles from Penzance to London.

Final Day of the Journey   Saturday 12 July

Parliament Square London

We listen to Premier Radio, we hear on the Tony Miles show with Lizzie about the Journey of the Christian faith and where we will be. Then we are off to Oxford Street by train with the memories of the Millennium Prayer Dance we did at Westminster Chapel still fresh in our memories. It is a lovely day weather wise. The train is packed with people already. Families with buggies, all manner of people. We stand until we can get seats and get off at Waterloo the end of the line. The station is packed with people toing and froing. There are cases being pulled everywhere. We walk out of the station and find a bus which takes us on the way to Oxford Street. We travel on the bus and alight.

We stop at a shop called La Pret Manger to have a snack, the phone rings it is Jeff from Stornoway telling us that Donna is out of hospital and home. Praise the Lord, what good news! We finish our meal and set forth, praying that Jesus will show us where to stand. We pass two horses with two guardsman sitting on them, one is moving his head up and down, the other is placid. We find Selfridges and put up our banner. The people are thronging past. There are many people here. It is a great missionary field. it is perhaps the greatest number of people we have seen of all shapes, colour and sizes. There are loads of rickshaws here, people going round. The buses come round one after another, taxies pass. Cars pass as Oxford Street is not pedestrianised. Workers regularly empty the bins. One man is busy reading the banner as he is working at the bins. People go past, looking.

A Christian couple come up to us and introduce themselves, they have heard about us on the Tony Miles Show on Premier Radio and they are very encouraging. Their names are Ben and Anna and they run the Yielded to Christ Mission Ministry. They give us a bookmark with John 3:16, 'For God so loved the World that He gave His one and only Son that whoever believes in

HIm (Jesus) shall not perish but have eternal life.' God loves you.

A man called Matt comes along, he is from the UK Fijian Service, Christian Mission Fellowship. A young lady hands us a card, she comes from ICEPI a company of which JESUS is the logo. They do Christian badges. She has come out this afternoon to tell people about these badges. A Jew comes up while we are chatting to Ben and Anna, he says that Jesus is a false prophet, he tells us that in the New Testament a false prophet would come and that was Jesus. We advise him to look at Psalm 22. We shake hands and he leaves. Many of our leaflets are given out as people are asking for them. We pray with Anna and Ben, then they leave.

The singing handyman goes past in his van, he has a mike as he slows down and stops, singing to us using his hands and then continues to drive telling us about his handy work, he is funny. There is a stone seat by us which wobbles, so people enjoy jogging up and down as they sit, eat and wait for the bus, A man sings and dances reggae as he waits for his bus. There is then consternation as a driver refuses to let a man on. He and two other men don't understand this. He complains to the next bus driver who comes along. The afternoon has been eventful. A man who is tipsy comes up and speaks saying that the Koran and the Bible are similar. He gives us a bar of chocolate and goes. An Asian man comes up, he is very interested and has a conversation with us. Another young man comes up and asks for a Bible. Some Chinese girls come up and ask us if we know of a church they can visit as they are in visiting London for a few days. We give them information about local churches and directions. At 5 o'clock we decide to leave, we walk down Oxford Street past Hamleys where a man is wearing a hat with a bubble gun, there are bubbles everywhere, they are all colours of the rainbow. We pass a lady in 1930s fashion on stilts with two men nearby, one telling us to roll up and see the lady with the longest legs while the other man stands beside her. We catch a bus and alight. We pass the place where the horses and guards were, there is now a guard standing.

We pass a statue of Edith Cavell, a nurse who died for her faith. Edith Cavell was a nurse in the first world war, she trained as a nurse in the Royal London Hospital, and in 1907 she went to Brussels in Belgium and was appointed matron at the Berkendael Institute. When the first world war started, the Red Cross took the hospital over. Edith then helped allied soldiers to escape from Belgium to the Netherlands which was neutral. She was arrested in 1915 and was executed for doing this. Edith knew the dangers but she wanted to help everyone whatever side of the war they were on. Edith Cavell before she died said, "Patriotism is not enough I must have no hatred or bitterness towards anyone."   We are reminded here of the command "Love Your Neighbour as Yourself."

In the square there are statues of Winston Churchill and other people in the square. We wait for our train to take us back to west London, having completed the Journey of the Christian Faith.

*Final stage of the Journey meeting up with local Christians
outside Selfridges Oxford Street*

Conclusion of the Journey of the Christian Faith

As we travelled the cities and towns we can see that there is a need for more Christians on the streets, proclaiming the Good News. There can be a nervousness which is understandable of going outside the church and meeting people and how they will react, our church circle is a world that we know and the people within it, they are our friends, our family in Christ, but Jesus wants to enlarge that family to bring others into His Kingdom because He created them and loves them as much as He loves us. Many people are grateful for us to go on the streets and seeing us in the market place, many have burning questions that they want answered. Christians do like meeting other Christians on the streets from other churches, to evangelise, it is right to encourage each other and for people to see us working together. We are mixing with the World just as Jesus did, we have all been along the road as unbelievers until Jesus touched our lives, we need to listen to these people's concerns and love them. People will not always go to church, the church needs to go to them giving the Gospel. We need places like the Father's House in Stornoway. People who are new to the faith are hurting, still getting over the past, single people with or without families need places like this to come and chat with the family of Jesus.

We as Christians must look at our lives and think about how can we give the Good News to others. Christians have busy lives, others have family but could we not tithe one hour to the Lord to go on the streets and tell others about Jesus. We could pray for our neighbours, our work colleagues or say to ourselves, 'I am going to tell someone about Jesus today,' there are endless opportunities to do this even if it is only five minutes. People who are housebound can pray for those evangelising on the streets. There are endless opportunities for us all. We have had prayer in our lives from people we do not even know and it is very encouraging for Christians to know that people are supporting them in prayer. We can encourage people to tune into Christian stations to hear about Jesus, Premier and UCB as well as local stations if people have them nearby and Christian bookshops, these are all good resources to get to know about Christianity. We have spoken to people on the streets to encourage them to use their Christian radio stations and let them hear about them. Sometimes a homeless person may have a radio that they can use.

The Church needs to be the Church of the street, in Stornoway the young people go out every weekend giving up their free time to evangelise to the people on the streets, it is not easy for them as some of the young people they reach out to are or have been school mates but they do it even if it is embarrassing, they are at an age where you like to fit in with friends and be part of the crowd. If these young people are willing to do this then surely those of us who are older can do so as well. The Street Pastors are a wonderful organisation who use Christians to go through the night telling people about Jesus until 2 o'clock in the morning. The Church needs to encourage Christians to go out and evangelise. Just as Jesus sent out His disciples, so must the Church. We have seen many churches being made into leisure centres, shops and temples as people have stopped going and the churches close. Jesus said "Go out and give the Good News to the Nations and make disciples of them. "Let the dead bury their dead, come follow me." We need passion to go out and a zeal for Jesus for people to be saved. We can stay in our churches and wait for people to come in but some will never enter. The young people need Jesus. We have stood with the banner, which they have looked at, and they are interested but they have no sense of direction. It would be lovely for them to see Jesus in dance, just as the young people were dancing for Jesus in Stornoway to show them that there is another way of life. Most people love debate and chatting. People are shy and will have problems approaching Christians. If we can remember what it is like going into the church for the first time, how we felt then we can imagine what it is like for someone to approach us.

When we find Jesus we are changing from one life to another, sometimes it can take time to adjust and for our old ways to slip away. One story which is very interesting is of the Roman Centurion in Matthew 8. The Roman Centurion went to Jesus, he had a servant who was very ill. Jesus said that He would go and heal him. The Centurion told Jesus that he was not deserving of Jesus coming into his home. He believed that if Jesus spoke the word that his servant would be healed. Jesus was amazed at the Centurions faith, "Go." Jesus said, "It will be done as you believed it would." The servant was healed at that very hour.

If we could have that faith to believe that Jesus will be with us on the streets to bring people into His Kingdom to tell them the Good News, we will have the boldness and the strength. Just as John Wesley in the 1750's and others have done. Billy Graham had the boldness to step out and preach the Gospel. We only have to ask and Jesus will do the rest.

Isaiah 61 "The Spirit of the Sovereign Lord is on me, because God anointed me to preach good news to the poor, to bind up the heartbroken, announce freedom for the captives and release from darkness for the prisoners." Jesus read this out aloud to the people when he went to Nazareth where He grew up and visited the local synagogue.

As Jesus died on the Cross for the Good News then surely we can go on the streets and tell people that He died, suffered pain, and rose from the dead. That they too can come out of a life of sin and into His Kingdom. Don't keep the Good News to yourself, share it with your family, friends and neighbours, you will be glad that you did and so will Jesus.

'I am the Vine, you are the branches. If a man remains in Me and I in him, he will bear much fruit, fruit that will last.' The fruit of the Good News.

Journey of the Christian Faith

We give thanks for this Book

as an opportunity to share with you

the 'Journey' that took place in 2008

as a Proclamation of the Christian Faith,

that God Loves this Nation, He desires to

bring His Love to all people through His

Only Son Jesus Christ by the Power of the Holy Spirit

Madeleine & Colin Windsor

Published by JC Ministries

www.jcministries.org.uk

020 8744 5005

Canaan Christian Bookshop Staines sends off the 'Journey of the Christian Faith' team with a blessing prayer

Andy Gilmour who is the founder and manager of
Canaan Christian Bookshop in Staines west London
supporting us in prayer before the Journey commenced

The 'Journey of the Christian Faith' office is based in west London and the Canaan Christian Bookshop is their local Christian Bookshop that provides the Mission in Hounslow Trust with resource material as to dvd's, books, cd's alongside other products. The Mission in Hounslow Trust has built up a strong relationship over the years with Andy Gilmour, founder and manager of the Christian Bookshop, as to 'Churches Together Groups' in west London (affiliated to Churches Together in England) and more recently with the online publication of 'West London Churches' newsletter. Canaan Christian Bookshop has been instrumental over the past three decades as to drawing together local churches in the Staines and surrounding area for such events as 'On the Move', HOPE08, church unity celebrations and other evangelistic outreaches. Andy was chair of Churches Together in Staines for several years. The Canaan Christian Bookshop endorses the 'Journey of the Christian Faith' as a step of faith and witness to the love of God through His Son Jesus Christ. '*Colin and Madeleine Windsor have served the Lord and His Church faithfully over the years through the Mission to Hounslow Trust and Churchlink, West London. We will be praying for them as they step out on this brave new initiative to travel this country reminding people about the message that brings real hope and salvation.*' Andy Gilmour.

www.canaanbookshop.co.uk

167

We would like to give appreciation to:

Mission in Hounslow Trust for sending us on this Journey

Daniel Cozens of 'Through Faith Missions' for supporting us with
prayer, encouragement and a Letter of Endorsement

www.t-f-m.org.uk

Premier Christian Radio for their letter of Endorsement
and the support that they have given us as to sharing about
the 'Journey' through their Radio Station

www.premier.org.uk

BBC local radio stations across the UK
Revival FM Scotland, UCB Radio,
Grampion4Gospel Radio, Transworld Radio,
Isles FM Stornoway, Cuillen FM Skye,
Eye Community Radio Leicester,
British Christian Media TV, Genesis - Revelation TV,
Baptist Times, New Life Magazine, Joy Magazine, Inspire Magazine,
Reachout Magazine N Ireland, Good News Catholic Magazine,
Christians Together Highlands & Islands Website Magazine,
New Wine Church Stornoway, Churches Together Stornoway,
Penzance Churches Together.

for enabling this 'Journey' to be shared
with up to 5 million people across the UK

The first phase of the Journey involved sharing
about the forthcoming 'Journey of the Christian Faith'.
This was done by taking part in interviews across the UK through
twenty three radio stations, Christian journals and contacting
thousands of Christian Churches & Christian ministries.

+++++++++++++++++++++++++

The second phase of the Journey involved actually travelling to
forty cities/towns throughout the UK during the summer of 2008, covering
4,500 miles by car and ferry over a seven week period, chatting to
people on the streets and sharing live on radio stations.

+++++++++++++++++++++++++

The third phase is to share our experiences to
churches/ministries across the UK as to
evangelism and Christian revival

+++++++++++++++++++++++++

CD's, DVD's & Press Releases are available:

Gospel4Grampian Community Christian Radio NE Scotland,
Cullin FM Skye, several BBC local radio stations, Premier Christian Radio,
Genesis - Revelation TV, Christian British Media TV and
press releases including the Baptist Times.

Copies of the interviews are available on request

+++++++++++++++++++++++++

'Journey of the Christian Faith' is currently featured on the
New Wine Church Stornoway Outer Hebrides website
http://www.newwinechurch.com

Click onto 'Fresh Bread Teaching' that is on the on left hand
tab to hear the Sunday 1 June 2008
40 Day Journey (Colin Windsor) message

Copies of the interviews are available on request